LONDON
UNDERGROUND
AT WAR

LONDON UNDERGROUND AT WAR

Nick Cooper

AMBERLEY

To all London Underground staff – past and present –

who keep the city moving.

First published 2014

Amberley Publishing
The Hill, Stroud
Gloucestershire, GL5 4EP

www.amberley-books.com

Copyright © Nick Cooper 2014

British Library Cataloguing in Publication Data.
A catalogue record for this book is available from the British Library.

ISBN 978 1 4456 2201 9
E-book 978 1 4456 2217 0

Typeset in 10pt on 12pt Sabon.
Typesetting and Origination by Amberley Publishing.
Printed in the UK.

CONTENTS

Tunnel vision – a section of newly constructed 'Tube' on the Piccadilly Line.

CHAPTER 1

BEGINNINGS

The London Underground was born of necessity. By the mid-nineteenth century the major railway companies had linked most parts of the country to London, but were prevented from venturing to the very heart of the city by Act of Parliament in the north and by high land prices north of the Thames in the south. Various railway companies had either sole possession or shared use of eleven mainline termini ringed around the capital, all desperate to project their lines further, both to link up with each other and, more importantly, to reach the ancient City of London, the financial powerhouse of the expanding Empire.

The only station actually within the boundary of the City was Fenchurch Street in the south-east, while to the north-east Bishopsgate lay just outside the border. To the north-west, King's Cross was about a mile and half from the edge of the City and Euston further still; London Bridge was on the other side of the Thames, close to the south bank of the river. The upshot of all this was that traffic – both human and freight – could go no further than these stations and instead had to transfer to the overloaded road network, which was clogged with horse-drawn cabs, coaches, omnibuses and carts.

One City commuter who found this situation intolerable was a solicitor, Charles Pearson. But he had a solution; if trains could not run into the City on the surface, then why not under it? Finding willing investors in both the City of London Corporation and the Great Western Railway Company (GWR), the North Metropolitan Railway Company was incorporated in 1853 with the intention of constructing a three-and-a-half-mile underground railway between the planned GWR terminus at Paddington and a new station at Farringdon Street, on the north-east edge of the City boundary. In between there would be five intermediate stations, including ones at Gower Street (Euston) and King's Cross.

Unfortunately, the easiest and cheapest way to construct the railway was also the most disruptive. To avoid the cost of demolishing buildings, roughly half of the line – west of Gower Street station – ran as much under existing roads as possible, using a method of construction that became known as 'cut-and-cover.' A deep wide trench was dug down the middle of the road, the brick tunnel built at the bottom of it, covered over again and the road re-laid. East of Gower Street, the line would be mostly in open cuttings. This was no bad thing given that the only motive power available was steam, so even the cut-and-cover sections needed frequent gaps to allow the smoke and fumes to escape.

Cut-and-cover sub-surface construction of the Metropolitan line passing King's Cross in 1861. *(JC)*

The line was ready by the end of 1862 and after the customary inspection and approval by the Board of Trade and a few days of trial working, the Metropolitan Railway opened for passenger traffic on Saturday 10 January 1863. The opening had been celebrated the previous Friday, but one conspicuously absent guest was Charles Pearson, who did not live to see his dream of an underground railway become reality, having died just four months previously.

Short though the original section of the Metropolitan was, by the end of 1864 it had been extended westward and then south to both South Kensington and Hammersmith, with a branch off the latter to Kensington (Addison Road). The following year saw an eastern extension to Moorgate Street and by the end of the decade a branch at Baker Street was making a tentative move into the north-western suburbs, reaching Swiss Cottage. To the south, the Metropolitan District Railway had opened between West Brompton and Blackfriars stations, with a link to the Metropolitan line proper at Brompton Road.

The rapid expansion of these sub-surface lines continued over the next twenty years until, by 1890, they had between them reached as far south as Wimbledon and Richmond, west to Hounslow and Ealing (from which a service to Windsor lasted two-and-a-half years before proving a bit too far) and north to Chesham. In the east, the acquisition and re-purposing of the pedestrian[1] Thames Tunnel – it was the first tunnel in the world built under a wide river – took both Metropolitan and District trains to New Cross. These extensions ran almost exclusively on the surface, since tunnels were not necessary further out where land was cheaper, but 1890 saw the arrival of a new player using a very different method of tunnelling.

In the mid-1860s, the engineer James Barlow developed a simplified variation of Marc Brunel's huge rectangular tunnelling shield, which had been used to construct the Thames Tunnel between 1825 and 1843. Rather than a brick tunnel, Barlow's would be composed of a series of 8-foot diameter rings formed from prefabricated curved cast iron segments, creating a continuous metal tube in which the track-bed would be laid; larger tubes would form the stations. When assembled, the outside diameter of the tunnels was slightly smaller than the circular tunnelling shield, so that the gap could be filled and sealed with liquid cement. This method of 'tube' construction – although much refined and now largely automated – remains in use to this day.

Although Barlow could not raise enough interest in a full railway, he tried out the basic principles by building a subway under the Thames between Tower Hill and Southwark – where there was no bridge at that time – with himself as engineer and his pupil James Henry Greathead as contractor. At each end of the tunnel there was a steam-powered lift to carry passengers 50 feet down to, or up from, the single 10-foot-long car that ran from one side of the river to the other on 2-foot 6-inch gauge track. Steam-powered cable haulage was used to move the car.

The Tower Subway officially opened on 2 August 1870, but never managed to carry enough passengers to cover the running costs and it proved mechanically unreliable.

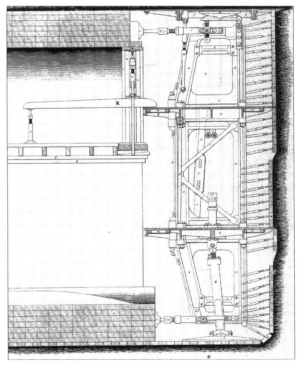

Marc Brunel's revolutionary tunnel shield for the Thames Tunnel. *(JC)*

The large 23-foot shield used to construct the platform tunnel at Turnpike Lane.

Extending the Piccadilly Line north: a running tunnel constructed using 12-foot Greathead Shield, near Manor House station site.

Tunnel segments being put in place with hydraulic rams.

Construction by hand where the new running tunnel meets the old at Finsbury Park.

Before long, the car and track were removed and the lifts replaced with spiral staircases in the shafts, making it into a simple pedestrian subway until rendered obsolete by the opening of Tower Bridge in1894.

Greathead continued to refine the tunnelling shield and in 1886 work began on the City & South London Subway (C&SLR), which consisted of twin 10-foot 2-inch diameter tubes running from Stockwell to Borough, then under the Thames to a northern terminus at King William Street in the City. Intermediate stations were at the Oval, Kennington and at Elephant & Castle. Tunnelling through the deep London clay it was still desirable, for legal reasons, to follow the line of the roads rather than go under buildings, and this resulted in a very tight curve and severe gradient at King William Street. This proved problematic for the early electric locomotives built for the line (it had originally been planned for cable haulage, with engine houses at Stockwell and the Elephant). When the time came to extend north to Moorgate, it was via new stations at London Bridge and Bank, bypassing King William Street completely, and thus it become the first underground station to ever close when the new stations opened on 25 February 1900. A further extension to Old Street, City Road and Angel followed in November 1901.

The next tube line to open was the one that managed to keep outside of the underground proper for almost a century of operation. The Waterloo & City (W&C) line was the brainchild of the London & South Western Railway (LSWR), which was hampered by having to terminate its trains at Waterloo, rather than the City. Plans for a full-size mainline tunnel under the Thames were more realistically and economically reduced to a self-contained two station shuttle tube railway between Waterloo and a station near the Bank of England, named – appropriately – 'City.' At 12-foot 1½-inches diameter, the tube was larger than the C&SLR, but the relative success with electric traction there soon put paid to the idea of using cable-haulage on the W&C and the innovative decision was taken to use motor cars and trailers, rather than locomotives and carriages. The rolling stock was built in the United States and assembled at the LSWR's Eastleigh Works. The line was built between 1894 and 1897 and opened on 11 July 1898.

Concurrent with the construction of the W&C was a third tube, the Central London Railway (CLR), which cut a horizontal line across the capital from Shepherd's Bush to a City terminus named 'Bank,' close to the C&SLR station. The tunnels were 11 feet 8¼ inches, but unlike the W&C the rolling stock consisted of UK-built cars hauled by a single heavy locomotive sourced from the United States.

Although the C&SLR and W&C had preceded it, the CLR was the tube railway that Londoners first embraced in a big way, thanks to its simple '2*d* to anywhere' fare structure (if it can even be called that) and an effective PR campaign. On 27 June 1900, the then Prince of Wales (later Edward VII) gave the new line the royal seal of approval by way of possibly the shortest opening speech for a railway ever:

> I have great pleasure in declaring the Central London Railway open. I am sure it will prove a great boon to our great city; and I think Sir Benjamin Baker, its engineer, is to be congratulated on the success with which he has carried out the undertaking. I ask you to drink with me – success to the Central London Railway!

The Waterloo & City platforms at City. The outbreak of war halted plans to link them to the Northern Line's Bank ticket hall with new escalators. *(JC)*

NOTICE TO QUIT.

The Fairy Electra (to Steam Locomotive Underground Demon). "Now they've seen me, I fancy your days are numbered."

[Centre of London Electric Railway opened by H.R.H. the Prince of Wales, Wednesday, June 27.]

The satirical magazine *Punch* gave its verdict on the new Central London Railway.

The CLR had established electricity as the traction of choice for underground railways and the satirical magazine *Punch* of 4 July hammered the point home with a cartoon showing the 'Fairy Electra' banishing the 'Steam Locomotive Underground Demon' with the words: 'Now they've seen *me*, I fancy *your* days are numbered.'

The next tube railway to open, in 1904, was unusual in having been built to take mainline-size trains to the City. The Great Northern & City Railway (GN&CR) ran from tube platforms below Finsbury Park station to Moorgate, with intermediate stations at Drayton Park, Highbury, Essex Road and Old Street. All were deep tube platforms, except Drayton Park, which was in an open cutting along with the line's depot.

The final three tube railways had all started out as separate ventures, but before construction began they had fallen under the control of the American tycoon Charles Tyson Yerkes. Born in 1837, he had had a chequered career as a stockbroker and financier in his home country, which culminated with him uniting the competing tramways in Chicago. He then set his eyes across the Atlantic and in 1900 bought up the dormant Charing Cross, Euston & Hampstead Railway (CCE&HR) company. He soon added the Brompton & Piccadilly Circus Railway (B&PCR), the Great Northern & Strand Railway (GN&SR) and the Baker Street & Waterloo Railway (BS&WR) to his portfolio, with an additional interest in electrifying the, by then ailing, Metropolitan along the way. In 1902 all of Yerkes' interests coalesced as the Underground Electric Railway Company of London (UERL), but he died in 1905 before any of the new tube lines opened.

The first to open, on 10 March 1906, was the BS&WR, running entirely in tube from Baker Street via Waterloo to Kennington Road (now Lambeth North), a temporary terminus until the opening of the last leg to Elephant & Castle (near the C&SLR station) on 5 August the same year. The line's elaborate name was soon popularly contracted to the 'Bakerloo.' Next came the Piccadilly line on 15 December the same year, running from Hammersmith to Finsbury Park, where the platforms lay alongside those of the GN&CR. At Hammersmith and Barons Court the surface line shared stations with the District, but went into tube for the rest of the route. As the Piccadilly was an amalgamation of the B&PCR and the GN&SR, a requirement to run to the Strand resulted in a semi-isolated station of that name on a short branch south of Holborn, although this didn't open until 30 November 1907.

The last of the Yerkes tubes to open was the CCE&HR on 22 June 1907, running from Charing Cross to Camden Town and then via separate branches to Golder's Green and Highgate (now Archway). The line included a station at Euston, which the C&SLR had already reached on 12 May 1907, when extended from Angel.

Two defining design features of the Yerkes stations are now so widely recognised that they are the only things that come close to the London Underground roundel as symbolising the system. The first are the surface buildings, almost all of which were constructed to the designs of the architect Leslie Green, with no two exactly alike, but all sharing common elements of large arched windows and clad in deep ox-blood red tiling. The other distinguishing feature is that each station featured a unique tiling pattern at platform level. The reason generally given is they would allow illiterate people to recognise their usual destination and while this may well have been the intention, the Elementary

No. 67, a Metropolitan Railway C class steam locomotive, dating from 1891 and, below, No. 10, a Metropolitan-Vickers electric locomotive built in the early 1920s. *(JC)*

Education Act 1870 had already mandated compulsory primary schooling between the ages of five and ten, meaning that by the time the stations opened there were few people under the age of forty who would not be able to read the station names (which were also incorporated into the tiling).

In 1914 the CCE&HR's Charing Cross terminus was extended a short distance to a new station on the Embankment. To enable a fast turnaround of trains, a loop tunnel took the southbound line partly under the Thames, before returning to join the northbound, and there was a single platform provided for both boarding and alighting. When the line was further extended in 1926 to Kennington (where a similar return loop was built and remains in use), a new southbound platform tunnel bisected the loop, which was sealed off with watertight bulkheads. It remained, however, a weak point in the system that almost proved the line's undoing during the Blitz (see Appendix 2). The opportunity was also taken to rename the stations in the Charing Cross area, which can best be summarised thus:

Line	Opened	06/04/1914	09/05/1915	Current
District	Charing Cross – 30/05/1870	Charing Cross		
Bakerloo	Embankment – 10/03/1906	Charing Cross [Embankment]	Charing Cross	Embankment
Northern				
Bakerloo	Trafalgar Square – 10/03/1906	Trafalgar Square	Trafalgar Square	Charing Cross
Northern	Charing Cross – 22/06/1907	Charing Cross [Strand]	Strand	
Piccadilly	Strand – 30/11/1907	Strand	Aldwych	Aldwych[2]

The early 1920s saw a flurry of activity on the CCE&HR and the C&SLR. The CCE&HR was extended from Golder's Green to Edgware between 1923 and 1924 and from Waterloo to join the C&SLR tunnels at Kennington. To allow for bigger rolling stock, the C&SLR tunnels were enlarged between 1922 and 1925, concurrent with the extension from Euston to join the CCE&HR tunnels at Camden Town in 1924.

The operational merger of the CCE&HR and the C&SLR called for a common rolling stock, which came with the 1923 introduction of what became known as Standard Tube Stock. At the time it had been intended to simply refurbish the original 'Gate Stock' used on the Bakerloo and Piccadilly lines, but when that proved almost as expensive as building new Standard Stock, the orders for the latter were increased to replace the older trains completely.

In 1926 the C&SLR line struck south, with an ambitious extension from Clapham

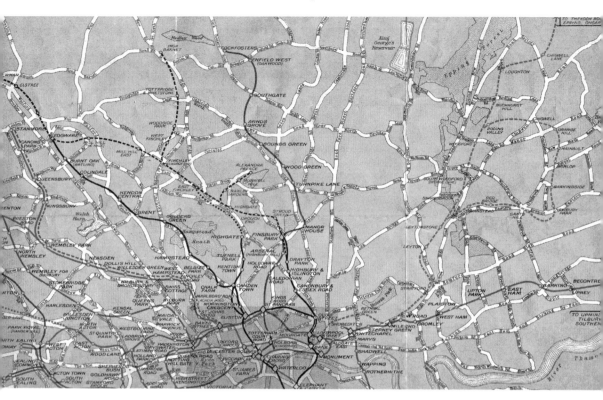

The 1935 New Works Programme envisaged extensions to the Northern and Central lines.

Common to Morden, all seven new stations being designed by the architect Charles Holden. Almost immediately before this, Holden had designed some of the First World War cemeteries of the Imperial (now Commonwealth) War Graves Commission, in an unornamented style described in the organisation's official history as, 'almost cruelly severe.'[3] Finished in the same white Portland stone as the cemeteries, the stations on the extension evoked the gleaming promise of functional modernism and his later design for the UERL's new headquarters at 55 Broadway was only marginally more decorative. Adorned with the work of leading contemporary sculptors such as Jacob Epstein and Henry Moore, when built it was the tallest office block in London. More austere, but no less radical, were Holden's functional brick designs for the Piccadilly line extension from Finsbury Park to Cockfosters between 1932 and 1933 and for the rebuilding of stations on the District line between Ealing Common and Uxbridge when the branch was taken over by the Piccadilly around the same time.

The creation of the London Passenger Transport Board in 1933 finally brought all public transport in the capital under central control, including all Underground lines – sub-surface and tube – as well as the trams, trolleybuses and buses (although progressive absorption of the latter stretched into 1934). The CLR became the Central line, the GN&CR the Northern City line and the CCE&HR and the C&SLR were merged as the

Morden–Edgware line. The Metropolitan District became simply the District line, while the Metropolitan, Bakerloo and Piccadilly were nominally unchanged. Only the W&C remained outside of public control, still part of the Southern Railway (SR), which had inherited the line upon its creation in 1923 as part of the grouping of Britain's railways.

In 1935 the LPTB formulated its New Works Programme (NWP) to modernise all of London's public transport. For the Underground, this meant the Bakerloo taking over the Metropolitan's slow lines between Finchley Road and Stanmore (the Metropolitan retained use of the parallel fast tracks) and extensions to the Central and Northern lines through a combination of new tunnels and connection to surface railways, which would be relinquished by their previous owners. The Central line eastern extension would involve tunnelling beyond the existing eastern terminus at Liverpool Street to join with LNER tracks at Stratford, encompassing the route to Ongar and the then-Fairlop Loop between Leytonstone and Woodford. A western extension would take the line from North Action to Denham via GWR tracks.

The Northern line extension – which became known as the 'Northern Heights' plan – was perhaps the lesser part of the NWP, although its component elements made it more complex and it was also largely based on the use of existing LNER tracks. These started at Finsbury Park and ran through two intermediate stations (Stroud Green and Crouch End) to one called Highgate, to the north of the Northern line terminus of same name. The line then split, with one branch running (via Cranley Gardens and Muswell Hill) to a terminus at Alexandra Palace and the other through East Finchley to Finchley (Church End), at

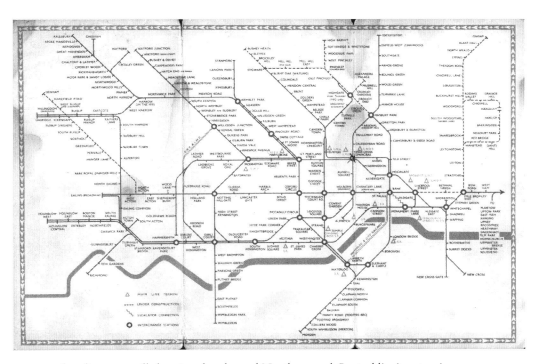

1940 pocket diagram, still showing the planned Northern and Central line's extensions.

The sleek lines of the 1935 Tube Stock and, below, the interior.

which point it divided once more. The double-track line continued to High Barnet, while a single-track led to an Edgware station just to the west of the Northern line one.

The plan was to extend the existing Northern line tunnel from its Highgate station – which would be renamed Archway – to new tube platforms directly below the LNER Highgate, making a new combined interchange. The tunnels would then rise to the surface either side of, and merge with, the LNER tracks to East Finchley. The whole surface line would be electrified to LPTB standards and the single-track line to LNER Edgware would be doubled and redirected into the LPTB station. The latter would be expanded with extra platforms to cope with the new connection and a subsequent northern extension of it, with new stations at Brockley Hill, Elstree South and Bushey Heath and a new depot between the last two. This last section had been planned since the mid-1900s and some work had already been done to allow for the extension in the mid-1920s. It is a sign of the times that the detailed plans for these new stations show that each would contain areas specifically set aside for Air Raid Precautions – the British organisation for civil defence against enemy bombing, formed in 1924.

If this would not make the Northern line complicated enough, it was also planned to run the Northern City line from Drayton Park to new high-level platforms at Finsbury Park, with a direct connection to the Alexandra Palace branch. Theoretically this would mean trains from Moorgate could run to Alexandra Palace, High Barnet, or Edgware/Bushey Heath, although in practice it seems that the intention was that only the trains coming from Camden Town would serve High Barnet. Either way, it was hoped that incorporating the Northern City would alleviate pressure on both the Bank branch and the overcrowded Camden Town junction.

The scale of the tube extensions called for additional trains, which led to the creation of two six-car trains of the experimental streamlined 1935 Tube Stock and then the simpler 1938 Tube Stock. Most of the latter went to the Bakerloo and Northern lines, with a small number augmenting the Standard Stock on the Piccadilly. In turn, the Central and Northern City lines inherited the Bakerloo's Standard Stock and most of the Northern line's.

In many respects the Underground's future was looking decidedly rosy, with the promise of new lines, new trains and modernised stations. Indeed, all that the New Works Programme promised would have given us a very different Underground system and city than we have today, had not a tyranny intervened.

Chapter 1 References:
1. It was originally designed for road traffic, but the approach ramps were never built.
2. Closed 30 September 1994. The surviving building still bears the original name.
3. Longworth, page 102.

Fiction: Casualties of blast and gas bombs being treated next to the Underground station entrance in the 1936 film *Things to Come*.

Reality: London Transport workers practice rail replacement under gas attack conditions.

CHAPTER 2

PRELUDES

In January 1915, at the height of the First World War, German airships crossed the English Channel to bomb the United Kingdom. Although they flew high enough to avoid anti-aircraft fire from the ground, they were susceptible to bad weather and navigation was so difficult that on one occasion they managed to bomb Kingston-upon-Hull, rather than the intended target of London. Towards the end of the year and into 1917, the German tactics changed to the use of Gotha G.IV and G.V aircraft, which were limited in their bomb load, but were more precise.

On 13 June 1917 a large force of Gothas attacked London in daylight, killing 162 people and injuring more than 400. Further daylight raids followed before a switch to night attacks. British attempts to shoot down the bombers were largely ineffectual, with most fighters being unable to climb high enough to engage them and the falling anti-aircraft shells being reckoned to cause as much damage as the German bombs. While never officially sanctioned, it was during both airship and bomber raids that Londoners first took to sheltering in the Underground system, although not in significant enough numbers to cause the authorities much concern.

Throughout the 1920s and early 1930s, tactical bombing was used on a minor scale in various colonial conflicts – most notably by the British in Iraq – while theories of strategic bombing were being developed by a number of the Western powers. At the same time, the evolution of the bomber was resulting in aircraft with ever increasing bomb loads, range and speed, but which would always be vulnerable to attack by enemy fighters. To counter this, defensive armament was increased to such a degree that it became the widely accepted belief that concentrated bomber formations could effectively hold off such attacks and thus the majority would reach their intended target. In this context, it came to be believed that a single 'super-raid' could effectively obliterate a modern city in a very short space of time. Speaking to Parliament in November 1932, the MP Stanley Baldwin warned:

> I think it is well also for the man in the street to realize that there is no power on earth that can protect him from being bombed, whatever people may tell him. The bomber will always get through and it is very easy to understand that if you realize the area of space. Take any large town you like in this island or on the Continent within the reach

of an aerodrome. For the defence of that town and its suburbs you have to split the air into sectors for defence. Calculate that the bombing aeroplanes will be at least 20,000ft in the air and perhaps higher and it is a matter of mathematical calculation that you will have sectors of from 10 to hundreds of cubic miles. Imagine 100 cubic miles covered with cloud and fog and you can calculate how many aeroplanes you would have to throw into that to have much chance of catching odd [bomber] aeroplanes as they fly through it. It cannot be done and there is no expert in Europe who will say that it can. The only defence is in offence, which means that you have got to kill more women and children more quickly than the enemy if you want to save yourselves.[1]

In 1934 the flamboyant film producer Alexander Korda managed to persuade H. G. Wells to adapt his 1933 novel *The Shape of Things to Come* for the cinema screen. In the film the fictional city of Everytown is seen passing through three phases of future history, starting with a surprise declaration of war by an unnamed enemy country on Christmas Eve 1940, the descent of the world into primitive medievalism in the late 1960s and finally a scientific and technological rebirth in the twenty-first century. Everytown is a clear stand-in for London, with a St Paul's Cathedral-like dome, a town hall resembling the Royal Exchange and a main thoroughfare akin to Piccadilly Circus. It also has an underground railway, with a modern entrance building on one side of the central city square and stairwells on the other. Contrary to real-life policy, when war breaks out the civilians are urged to shelter in the railway tunnels in the event of a surprise air raid. When such an attack happens, we see a panicked crowd scramble down the stairwells as gas and high explosive bombs explode around them. By 1966 the bedraggled survivors are living in the ruins of Everytown, including the old tunnels.

Although *Things to Come* was fiction, the outbreak of the Spanish Civil War in July 1936 soon saw civilian populations attacked by modern bombers for real. Even before the infamous raid on Guernica in 1937, German Legion Condor and Italian Aviazione Legionaria bombers – supporting General Franco's fascist rebels – attacked the besieged capital of Madrid in November 1936. An English-language[2] poster produced by the Spanish Republican government to raise awareness and support abroad was headed: 'MADRID – THE 'MILITARY' PRACTICE OF THE REBELS,' above a mortuary photograph of the body of a child killed in one such raid, and the stark warning: 'IF YOU TOLERATE THIS, YOUR CHILDREN WILL BE NEXT.'

During a period of just under forty-eight hours from 16–18 March 1938, the Aviazione Legionaria carried out a series of thirteen air raids against the Spanish government-held city of Barcelona. Several months later the British war correspondent John Langdon-Davies published an account of the attack, suggesting that it amounted to a deliberate and systematic experiment in the aerial bombardment of a civilian population, in preparation for a future conflict against the British, targeting London in particular. The three crucial factors were varying the times between each raid, between 1 hour 29 minutes and 8 hours 18 minutes, the aircraft gliding in from very high altitude with their engines off and the use of large capacity high explosive bombs.

Unable to detect the gliding aircraft – which Langdon-Davies dubbed 'silent approach' – with the pre-radar acoustic methods of the time, the first that the government forces knew of an attack was the bombs themselves exploding, so the single-note air raid sirens only sounded *after* this had happened. Coupled with the variance of the time between raids, this provoked extreme anxiety and confusion in the population, who could not know when the next attack would occur, or even whether one had started or finished. Langdon-Davies termed this 'suspense without danger.' Meanwhile, the use of higher capacity bombs than had been dropped on the city previously proved just how much more effective they were in destroying urban targets. Earlier raids had been limited to bombs in the 50–100 kg range; the March 1938 raids involved ones of 250 and 500 kg, which had a wider blast radius and also produced a secondary 'suction' effect – caused by atmospheric pressure re-exerting itself after the initial outward blast – that literally pulled the front off the nearby buildings.

Although radar obviously made 'Silent Approach' obsolete, Langdon-Davies speculated as to the effect of an attack on London:

> If we look at the map of Barcelona we see that the conditions in the Corts are not unlike what would happen if a bomb fell in Piccadilly Circus near the Café Royal. Such a bomb would deposit most of the Piccadilly Hotel and the buildings opposite into the street. [It] would damage the steel drum supporting the Circus over the tube station ... [and] would disturb the tube station and escalators beneath the surface.[3]

While Piccadilly Circus was never damaged in this way, it accurately predicts what happened to Bank station in January 1941 (see Chapter 6).

Official Spanish government posters advanced the idea of the Barcelona Metro, which had opened in 1924, as a secure refuge from bombing, but Langdon-Davies considered its largely cut-and-cover tunnels to be unsuitable:

> The crowds in the Metro were such that everybody had to stand all night long for two successive nights wedged body to body; (Yet the Metros are not safe from bombs; people would have been safer in their own homes.) For several weeks after it was necessary to open trains on one side only, so as to leave the other platforms for the campers who would not leave.[4]

He went on to quote one resident who described the appalling conditions:

> I tried to go into the Metro. But that was terrible. So many people had gone down that there was no room for anyone to sit down or lie down. They stood wedged there hour after hour. Imagine children crying, with the bodies of older people stifling them; and not only the children – women got hysterical. And the smell; people urinating and defecating as they stood, because there was nothing else they could do. It went on like that all those days.[5]

Langdon-Davies reckoned that of the twenty or so stations on the three line Metro, around half were suitable as air raid refuges and 'those who crowd to the less safe underground stations go to a death trap.' He also noted:

There are mysterious rumours of great underground tunnels. It is true that two underground lines have been excavated but never used for transport. It is rumoured that they are used as ammunition dumps. It is certain they are not used for refuges.[6]

The unused tunnels had been built under the Carrer de Balmes when the street was extended between 1921 and 1929, but were not incorporated into the Metro system until the 1950s. During the Civil War, they were indeed used to store munitions – being divided into four sections separated by steel blast doors – so the rumours were right.

Langdon-Davies was critical of British Air Raid Precautions (ARP) and in particular the heavy emphasis on the threat of poison gas. Despite it being available, it had not been used in Spain, but more importantly the use of high explosive bombs made a mockery of the idea that ordinary people could construct, and survive in, gas-proof rooms in their own homes. Instead he advocated the construction of large purpose-built gas and blast-proof public shelters, but also the need for protected underground arterial roads across London, so vital traffic could circumvent bomb debris-strewn streets.

Having seen that a sense of helplessness and lack of inclusion had bred anxiety and panic within Barcelona's civilian population, he suggested that Londoners should be encouraged to take on specific wartime duties and that the public shelters should include proper work

Above: In 1939 the Underground was used in the evacuation of London's children.
Left: The LT ARP manual was almost entirely composed of advice on dealing with gas attack, rather than the effects of high explosives.

facilities to give those using them something useful to do, rather than simply sit and fret their way through air raids. He advised the creation of a centralised Blood Transfusion Service, as the one in Barcelona had not only provided the necessary supplies to meet the surgical needs of the city, but had also engendered a positive sense of involvement in the city's defence on the part of the donors.

He warned, though, that one of the greatest detriments to morale was actually anti-aircraft fire, since many found it indistinguishable from the enemy bombing, as they had in London during the First World War. Every effort should be made to both minimise such firing when there were no definite target and to educate the public to be able to tell the difference between 'our guns' and 'their bombs.' He considered that, 'without suggesting that gas masks are going to be quite useless it is at least possible to suggest that ear protectors and sound deadeners will be as useful.'

In late September 1938, at the height of the Munich Crisis, ARP measures were activated. Gas masks were distributed, buildings were buttressed with sandbags, trees and other street obstacles were whitewashed to be more visible in the blackout and thousands of Londoners spontaneously participated in the rush to dig trenches for shelter against air attack in the capital's common land, parks, public gardens and squares. On Hampstead Heath, Hackney Downs, Lincoln's Inn Fields and in the grounds of St Guy's Hospital and the playing fields of Westminster School – to name but five – no patch of open ground was too sacred, except perhaps for the pitch at Wembley Stadium.

As the threat of the dreaded 'super raid' seemed imminent, the LPTB's hand was forced on one particular matter. There had long been concerns that a heavy enough bomb exploding in the river bed of the Thames could cause the collapse of one or more of the Underground tunnels passing underneath it and the Northern and Bakerloo lines at Charing Cross were, due to their shallow depth, thought to be particularly vulnerable. With no time for any other alternative, the affected stations were closed at 8 p.m. on 27 September in order for the tunnels either side of the river to be sealed with solid concrete plugs. The following LPTB statement was issued to the press:

> The Board regrets to announce that the Bakerloo and Hampstead [sic] Lines at Charing Cross must be closed at 8 p.m. tonight for urgent structural works until further notice. The Bakerloo Line will run from Queens Park to Piccadilly Circus only. The Hampstead Line from Edgware and Highgate to Strand. The Morden Line will continue to run to the City but not to the West End.[7]

See Appendix 2 for more details of these measures.

Having reached an agreement with Adolf Hitler, Benito Mussolini and Édouard Daladier, Prime Minister Neville Chamberlain returned to Britain. After his aircraft landed at Heston Aerodrome, he promised 'peace for our time', publicly at least, while privately hoping he had bought the nation time to re-arm. Britain would not be ready to fight Germany in 1939, but it would be more ready than it had been in 1938. Having secured the largely German-speaking Sudetenland from Czechoslovakia by negotiation, Hitler would wait barely six months before taking the rest of the country by force.

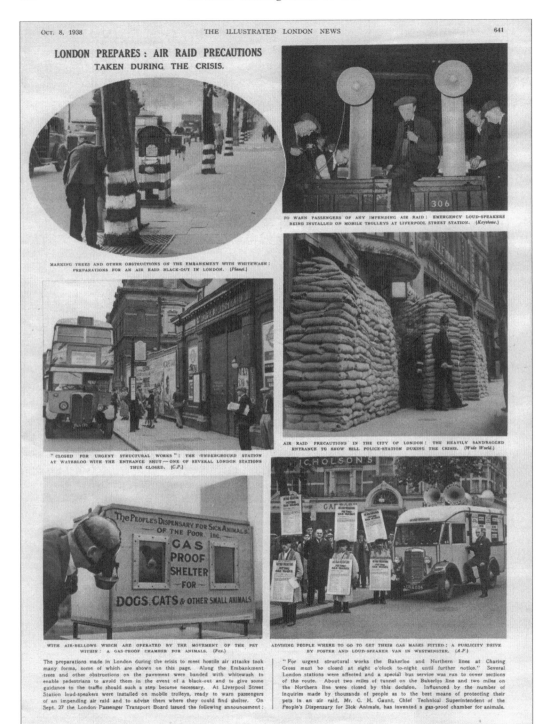

The Illustrated London News, 8 October 1938.

The immediate crisis averted, the concrete plugs protecting the sub-Thames tunnels were drilled out and services resumed, but the powers that be were forced to confront the reality that the threat from Germany was real and that Britain's civilian population was woefully unprotected. However, the Underground soon became the focus of a different form of attack. On 3 February 1939, as part of the Irish Republican Army's S-Plan campaign on the British mainland, suitcases containing bombs were deposited at the left-luggage offices at Tottenham Court Road and Leicester Square Underground stations. They exploded the next morning, causing extensive damage and injuring two people, although not fatally. Twenty-three men were subsequently tried for these and other attacks. Two were acquitted, but the rest were found guilty and received prison terms of between eighteen months and seventeen years.

On 1 September 1939 German forces invaded Poland and launched the first of many air raids against Warsaw. Although Britain did not declare war for another two days, the pre-planned evacuation of London's school children began immediately, with many converging via the Underground system on Edgware, where fleets of buses whisked them away to the relative safety of the countryside.

On the same day the Northern line platforms at Waterloo, Charing Cross, Trafalgar Square and Strand (the latter two being the Bakerloo and Northern platforms of the current Charing Cross) stations were again closed to allow the same preventative sealing as in the previous year. This was done some 20 feet down the tunnels to allow for the installation of proper movable flood-gates, after which the temporary blockages were removed. Waterloo reopened on 16 December and Charing Cross and Strand the following day. The remnants of these flood-gates can still be seen at the ends of the platforms nearest to the river.

In addition to the vulnerability of the sub-Thames tunnels, it had been determined that a number of other stations might be flooded if large capacity water mains in the immediate vicinity were fractured by enemy bombing. Because the threat was from the surface, rather than water coming from the running tunnels, temporary concrete plugs were used to block entrances close to street level, while flood-gates were installed in the low-level passageways below. The following stations were closed on 7 September for this work to be done:

Arsenal (to 1 December 1939)
Balham
Bank – Northern line platforms only (to 18 May 1940)
Bond Street
Chancery Lane
Clapham Common
Green Park (to 1 December 1939)
Hyde Park Corner (to 8 December 1939)
Kings Cross (to 17 November 1939)
Knightsbridge (to 1 December 1939)
Maida Vale
Marble Arch
Old Street

Oval
Oxford Circus (open for interchange between lines)
Tottenham Court Road (open for interchange between lines)
Trinity Road [Tooting Bec]

Later on, similar flood-gates were installed at other stations such as Baker Street, Holborn, Leicester Square, London Bridge, Moorgate and Tooting Broadway, many of which can still be seen in situ (the ones in the passageways between the Piccadilly and Northern line platforms at Leicester Square were tiled over during a refurbishment several years ago, but remain conspicuous).

Other wartime measures, although not being as disruptive, certainly did not make journeys for the hapless passenger any easier. Stations were blacked out and the windows of trains received a fabric net covering, secured by a strong varnish. This served both to reduce night-time light leakage and to minimise the separation of the glass into potentially lethal shards in the event of being shattered by blast. Only a small diamond or circle of clear glass was left for passengers to try to work out where they were. Somewhat improbably, station names were removed or reduced on the roundels at certain open-air platforms, for fear that they could be seen and read from enemy aircraft and thus used for navigational purposes.

Disruptive though it had been, the Munich Crisis was one thing, but the actual outbreak of war was another matter entirely. While existing lines were vital to the life and commerce of the capital, the New Works Programme had to be reassessed. With the country facing the prospect of possibly having to fortify itself in a very literal sense, large scale construction projects had to be justified, even those already in progress.

In the case of the Northern Heights part of the Plan, the new tunnels linking Archway (Highgate) to the LNER surface tracks were already complete and East Finchley had been served by Northern line trains since 3 July that year, although the new Highgate low-level platforms were not yet ready, so trains were non-stopping there. Completing the electrification of the rest of the East Finchley–High Barnet branch could be done within a reasonable timescale and so was allowed to proceed. Services on the branch began on 14 April 1940.

In contrast, although some preliminary work had been done on the Finsbury Park–Alexandra Palace branch, it could not be completed quickly enough under wartime conditions. LNER steam services would continue to work the branch, but with no Underground trains running from Finsbury Park, there was also little justification for continuing with the conversion of the single track from Finchley Central to Edgware, despite some preliminary work having already been done. The sole exception was the recognised utility of Mill Hill East station due to its close proximity to the large Inglis Barracks, so electrification of the single line as far as there proceeded, with the branch opening on 18 May 1941. Steam freight services continued to run along the un-electrified tracks to Edgware.

Similarly, but on a smaller scale, the Southern Railway was in the middle of a number of improvements to the Waterloo & City line. On 9 September it was decided between the company and the LPTB that a planned triple-bank of escalators to be built at City/Bank,

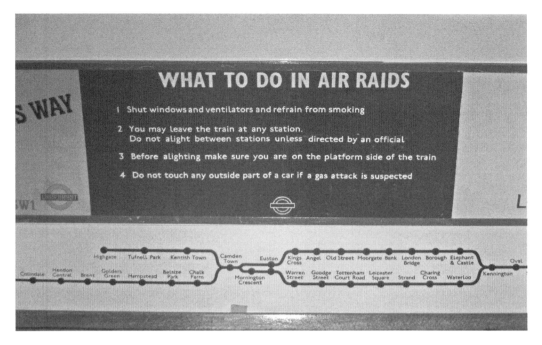

Advertising within the trains was used to give advice to wartime passengers.

to replace the single sloped pedestrian passageway down to the W&C platforms from the Central line ticket hall, would not go ahead. It would be another twenty years before the 'nasty slope' at the station was augmented with an inclined 'Trav-o-Lator' in a parallel tunnel, but work on modernised signalling was too pressing, as was the introduction of new trains. Eventually designated as BR Class 487, the English Electric rolling stock introduced in October 1940 in many ways surpassed the clean modernist lines of the Underground's own 1938 Tube Stock and lasted until the 1990s. Concerned that the W&C's own power supply could be knocked out by enemy action, the SR requested on 12 September that the LPTB might be able to arrange an emergency alternative and it reflects both wartime co-operation and the degree of cordiality between the two bodies that this work was agreed and completed by 11 October.

One constant thread running through official considerations, however, was that under no circumstances should the London Underground itself be used as a refuge from enemy attack, except in the most immediate of emergencies (alighting passengers could hardly be pushed out of the stations and into an actual air raid!). This did not, however, mean that certain 'non-active' infrastructure could not find a wartime use. The closing of a number of deep tube stations in the 1920s and 1930s had already provided the makings of the start of the deep shelter provision the press and certain political activists had been demanding and which even the public itself still hoped for. The same also applied to the incomplete tunnelling done for the eastern extension of the Central line and all of these will be covered in the following two chapters.

The wartime demand on manpower for the armed services necessitated a massive increase in women working on the Underground network, even in roles that would have previously been inappropriate for them, including trackside maintenance, ticketing, signals, as well as train and line cleaning.

With conscription introduced, while railway work was a 'reserved occupation,' so many London Underground employees volunteered for military service that the workforce was severely depleted. Pragmatism over-rode years of prejudice and the LPTB turned to a ready and willing source of labour. Just as their mothers, aunts and older sisters had done twenty-five years previously, the women of London donned uniform or overalls, rolled up their sleeves and filled the gaps in London Transport's decimated ranks.

On 10 May 1940 German forces invaded France and the Low Countries. Four days later, as remnants of the Dutch army valiantly attempted to resist the German Blitzkrieg, the Luftwaffe fell upon Rotterdam – which effectively had no anti-aircraft defences – killing 900 people and destroying the medieval heart of the city. Militarily questionable, the raid was a stark object lesson in how much the power of aerial bombing had progressed since Madrid, Guernica, Barcelona and even Warsaw.

The London Blitz began on 7 September 1940, two weeks before H. G. Wells's seventy-fourth birthday. Even though he had confidently predicted the destruction by air of his proxy-London of Everytown in *Things to Come*, like so many Londoners – adopted as well as born – he resolutely refused to leave the capital. Instead he volunteered for fire-watching duties, spending many a night on the roof of the elegant Regent's Park terrace where he lived. It was to be a long war.

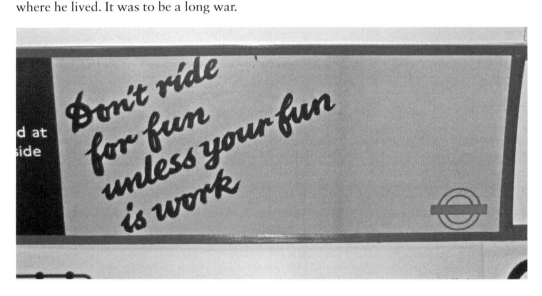

Chapter 2 References:
1. *The Times:* 'Mr Baldwin on Aerial Warfare.' 11 November 1932, page 7.
2. A French version was also produced.
3. Langdon-Davies, 1938, pages 77–78.
4. Langdon-Davies, 1938, pages 46
5. Langdon-Davies, 1938, page 119.
6. Langdon-Davies, 1938, page 121
7. CAB 21/773.

Above, 55 Broadway in an advert from 1928.

Right: The disused Aldwych Station today, showing the original name sign as Strand Station. Below: Early ad hoc sheltering on the station escalators. There was little protection in the event of the station being hit.

Lower concourse areas were also vulnerable. The platform tunnels were safer, but some space had to be left for bona fide passengers.

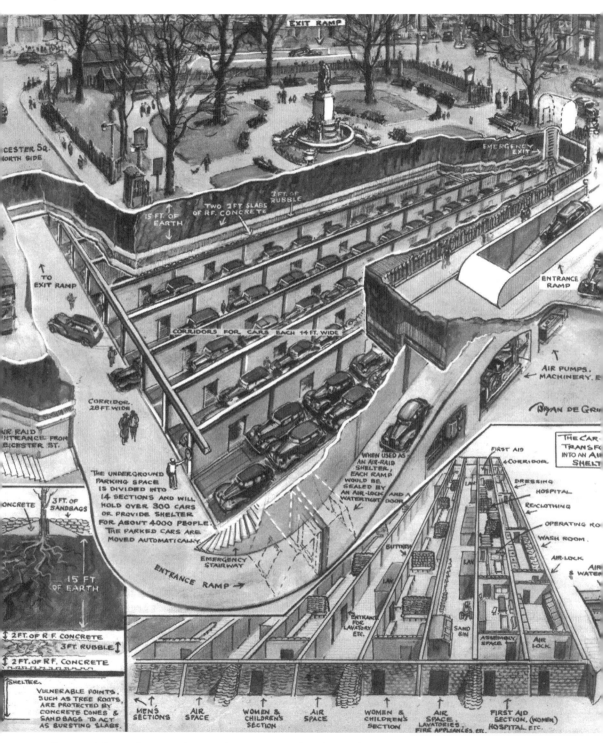

Proposal for underground carpark come air raid shelter under Leicester Square.

CHAPTER 3

SHELTERED LIVES

The Munich Crisis was a wake-up call alerting the nation to the threat to the capital in the event of war and in particular the availability – or rather lack – of 'deep shelter' provision for the civilian population; the hastily-dug trenches of September 1938 were clearly little more than a straw-clutching exercise. Immediately following the Crisis, newspapers were littered with fanciful artist's impressions of increasingly ambitious and grandiose schemes to convert London's parks and squares into improbably vast and expensive air raid shelters.

One relatively modest idea was to build a subterranean car park under Leicester Square (ironically where *Things to Come* had its 1936 premiere), designed to be converted in time of war into a shelter, complete with hospital, washrooms and gender-segregated dormitories. In peacetime it would no doubt have appealed to car-owning theatre- and cinema-goers, but one wonders about its usefulness in the event of a surprise attack if filled with vehicles and therefore a lot of petrol.

At the other end of the scale was a monumental plan for a huge multiple-level shelter under Hyde Park, with not only pedestrian access to the Piccadilly line station, but also deep level platforms for direct connection to the main lines. It was suggested that this would allow the speedy and safe evacuation of shelter occupants to the country, raising the question of what the rest of the structure was actually for. Why build a shelter capable of housing tens of thousands of people, only to empty it as quickly as possible?

A constant agitator for civilian deep shelter construction was the *Daily Worker*, the newspaper of the British Communist Party, bolstered by the object lessons of the Spanish Civil War. They found a willing advocate in the geneticist J. B. S. Haldane, who was a vocal supporter of deep shelter provision for all. Writing for the newspaper in June 1938, he confidently suggested that tunnels suitable for sheltering could be built for £12 5s per person (£1,823 now). This compared to estimates of between £30 and £50 per head in other schemes.[1] In a later issue, the newspaper confidently asserted:

The proceeds of one year's rent would provide absolute safety from air attack for all the 8,000,000 people in Greater London. The same job could be done for the amount paid out in every 4½ months to those rich people who live on our National Debt.[2]

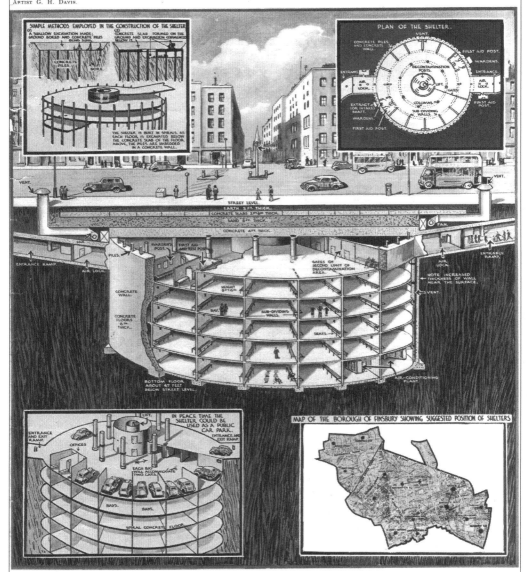

Ambitious plans for spiral shelters in Finsbury.

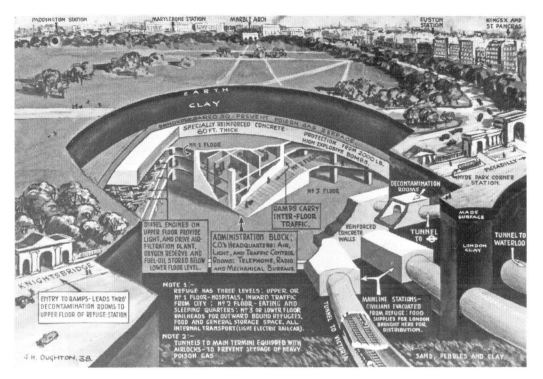

The massive shelter proposed for Hyde Park.

Away from such flights of fancy, the reality for the authorities was more mundane, pragmatic and, most importantly, affordable. Do-it-yourself Anderson shelters were to be distributed to those with gardens in which to assemble them, while elsewhere, quietly and largely unnoticed, locations suitable for conversion to air raid shelters were identified and surveyed and plans drawn up for surface shelters where they were the most practical alternative.

With the outbreak of war in September 1939 the need for public shelter provision gained added impetus, but one particular borough had been blessed with a piece of historical good luck. Southwark Council had initially looked into two schemes, one of which was an underground car park – presumably not dissimilar to those championed by the press – but both would essentially require complete construction from scratch, when time was short. A much more inviting proposition was the pair of disused C&SLR tube tunnels running from Borough to the abandoned King William Street station. This was not actually a new idea, as it had been first suggested by a reporter writing for the *Star* newspaper on 17 March 1936,[3] after a visit to the disused station. On 10 November 1939 the same journalist reported that conversion of the tunnels between Borough station and the Thames would begin the next day. The work would cost £40,000 (£5.7 million today) and take around three months to complete. The estimate included ventilation, a first aid post and construction of six new pedestrian entrances to the tunnels. New bulkheads were installed at the Thames end; others had already been fitted at the southern ends of the tunnels at the time of the Munich Crisis.

When work began in January 1940 it had been expected to cost £50,000 (£6.5 million) – most of which would be reimbursed by the government – but by 1943, the total spent was £105,628 (£12 million). This included a 'token' annual rental of £100 (£14,000) to the LPTB, which had inherited ownership of the tunnels from the C&SLR and were presumably eager to see the conversion, as it would make illicit sheltering at Borough or London Bridge stations less likely.

The shelter opened on 24 June 1940, a few days after the first sporadic bombing in the London area. It was opened at 8 p.m. each evening, by which time long queues had usually built up. Each of the six new entrances could admit 300 people per minute, with the capacity for the shelter being 14,000 without overcrowding.

Across the river, the King William Street station building had vanished when the surrounding land was redeveloped as an office block called Regis House in 1933, but although this had resulted in the capping of the original lift shaft, the emergency stairs remained, connected to the basement of the new building. In early 1940, the owners of Regis House took out a lease on the single platform tunnel as far south as the crossover where it separated into the two running tunnels. With the addition of a mezzanine floor and a new staircase connected to King William Street House (on the other side of the road from Regis House), the tunnel was converted into a private air raid shelter with a total capacity of 2,000 people.

In early 1940 Stepney Borough Council also availed themselves of some disused Underground infrastructure to meet their public shelter needs. St Mary's station, situated between Aldgate East and Whitechapel on the District line, had closed on 30 April 1938. Unlike the King William Street and the C&SLR tunnels, however, the platforms were cut-and-cover and trains still ran through them. This necessitated the building of a wall along the platform edge, the installation of a false ceiling sufficient to prevent bomb penetration or collapse and a dividing floor to double the platform area. The shelter had capacity for 1,171 people, with bunks for 475, and opened in early 1941. Even before conversion work was completed, however, the original surface building was so badly bomb-damaged on 22 October 1940 that it had to be demolished. The basic brick replacement surface structure lasted until 19 April 1941, when it too was damaged in an air raid, with significant loss of life (see Appendix 1). By 24 October 1941 the final cost of the conversion was £9,121 (£1.13 million), of which £1,000 was work done by the LPTB.[4]

In June 1940, the City Corporation opened a shelter in two unfinished 730-foot siding tunnels built at Liverpool Street for the Central line extension. They were capable of housing 2,500 people, but to begin the conditions with were basic in the extreme. Bunks were fitted in October 1941 and eventually facilities improved.[5]

Although there was some light bombing of central London in late August 1940, the Blitz proper did not begin until the first massed attack on the afternoon of 6 September 1940, mostly targeting the areas around the docks. On the evening of 8 September, despite the efforts of police, troops and LPTB staff to keep them out, a large crowd of shelterers gained access to Liverpool Street station,[6] and on 11 September, 2,000 made it into Holborn station (where the *Daily Worker* claimed there was room for another 4,000).

Borough Tube Station today - the shelter tunnels still run under the road to the right of this picture. Below: A plaque at the station commemorates the site of the wartime shelter.

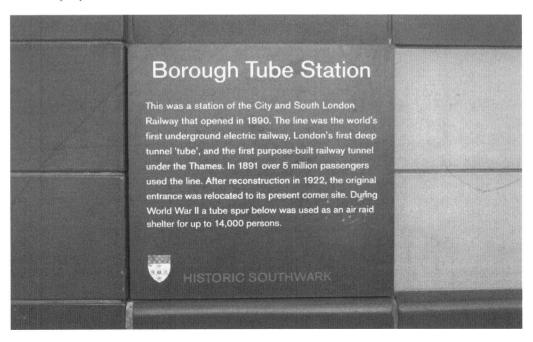

Borough Tube Station

This was a station of the City and South London Railway that opened in 1890. The line was the world's first underground electric railway, London's first deep tunnel 'tube', and the first purpose-built railway tunnel under the Thames. In 1891 over 5 million passengers used the line. After reconstruction in 1922, the original entrance was relocated to its present corner site. During World War II a tube spur below was used as an air raid shelter for up to 14,000 persons.

HISTORIC SOUTHWARK

Two modern troglodytes arriving at the station in style. And to judge by the quantity of luggage, they are resigned to spending many hours on some platform complete with southern aspect and hot and cold draughts

Platforms can become uncommonly hard after an hour or two, but a few cushions applied to the parts where it hurts the most are a great help. These youngsters have become experts at making a little comfort go a long way

Good platform positions are now sought as eagerly as were the front rows of the pit and gallery in the days of peace. And the crowd makes its way in with the well-disciplined eagerness of the theatre queue

London Carries On . .

UNDERGROUND LIVES

ADAPTABILITY has always been a prominent ingredient in the make-up of the Londoner and never has it been so greatly in evidence as in these stressful days.

Now that Hitler has deluded himself into thinking that the morale of the civil population is less than that of our fighting forces, the man in the street has accepted the Nazi challenge.

And each in his own way is finding the answer to the ruthless, cold-blooded bombing of the humble homes of London.

In the Underground stations is to be found protection from the bombs of the Nazis, and here Londoners come when night falls. Armed with pillows, blankets, food and newspapers, they settle down for a night's rest with a cheerful patience.

Londoners must carry on tomorrow and they mean to be fit to do their part in bringing about the overthrow of the Nazi regime.

Stairway squatters obey the injunction to "keep on the side" when they take up their places for the night—or anyhow, for some part of it. Their quarters may not be the acme of comfort, but at least they are warm, light and safe

Long before the last train has rumbled off into the darkness of the tunnel, the squatters have taken up their places along the length of the platform sitting in rows two or three deep. Their patience is exemplary, and they are a quiet and orderly crowd who, in the words of a music hall song famous some years ago, " are watching all the trains come in, hearing the porters shout. When they've watched all the trains come in—they watch all the trains go out"

Naturally, the inner man must be studied, so the unexpired portion of the day's rations is taken underground to help the squatters through the long hours of night vigil. Families often pool their foodstuffs and their drinks

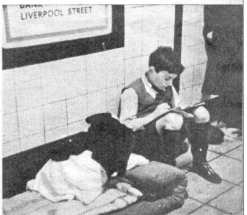

Raids or no raids, homework must be done before turning in for a night's rest on the eastbound platform. And if only the teacher has set an essay on London's Underground; How It Works; well, here is one expert pupil

In subsequent years, actions such as these have been presented as the ordinary public taking their destiny in their own hands in the face of callous official indifference, yet at the time wider opinions were more ambivalent. In the early days, the press referred to shelterers as 'campers' at best and 'Tube squatters' at worst. Much of the animosity seems to have been channelled against men – real or imagined – who were supposedly cowering in the shelters, rather than doing voluntary war work (ARP, fire-watching, etc.). Towards the end of September, the LPTB issued a poster, bluntly stating:

TO ALL ABLE-BODIED MEN
The trains must run to get people to their work and to their homes.
The space at the tube stations is limited.
Women, children and the infirm need it most
Be a man and leave it to them.[7]

It was later estimated that women and children formed the bulk of shelterers – 55 per cent and 15 per cent respectively – leaving only 30 per cent men. Given that many of the latter will have been elderly, it is understandable that the above poster caused a great deal of resentment, and may even have fostered the idea that too many men were using the shelters. Consequently it was not used after the end of October 1940.[8]

Although many stations were rapidly becoming *de facto* air raid shelters, this clearly wasn't enough for the *Daily Worker*, which on 13 September perniciously claimed:

Southwark Tenants' Defence Association has discovered that the huge tunnel, now being used by thousands of people from all over London as an air raid shelter, extends at least as further mile as far as the Elephant and Castle district. At present this further tunnel, which can hold many thousands more people, is blocked by a brick wall.

This was completely untrue. The Southwark shelter extended to where the former C&SLR tunnels branched off to London Bridge, just north of Borough station. As converted, the southern limits of the two disused tunnels were just short of the step-plate junctions where the new tunnels to London Bridge branched off and where concrete bulkheads had been installed during the Munich Crises. The bulkhead in the northbound tunnels was under the junction of Borough High Street and Tabard Street, only 100 yards beyond the station; in the southbound tunnel it was near Chapel Court, about 250 yards from the station. The rest of the original tunnels did indeed extend to the Elephant, but they still had trains running through them! This was, though, a classic example of how false rumours were rife at the time.

On 19 September 1940 *The Times* reported that the Ministries of Home Security and Transport had issued the following appeal:

The facilities provided by the Tubes are of vital importance to London's transport and particularly so in these days. An urgent appeal is therefore made to the good sense of the public and particularly to able-bodied men, to refrain from using Tube stations as air raid shelters.[9]

The whole problem is now being reviewed by the authorities concerned with a view to seeing whether some practical plan can be evolved for providing a measure of shelter outside rush hours which will not impair the essential use of the Tubes for traffic purposes. The problem is, however, a very difficult one, particularly since at the rush hours, which extend to 8 p.m., the whole of the available space is required for traffic purposes.

On Saturday 21 September, however, the same newspaper reported:

The section of tube between Aldwych and Holborn stations may soon be closed to traffic to enable it to be converted into an air-raid shelter. The scheme is under discussion between the Minister of Home Security and the London Passenger Transport Board. The section is about one-third of a mile long and is a branch of the Piccadilly line.[10]

This news caused some consternation in government circles, since it clearly contradicted the previous announcement and indeed what was assumed to be agreed policy. No less surprised was the Prime Minister, Winston Churchill, who had been in favour of some use of the Underground for sheltering, but had been assured that it was not feasible. He demanded explanations from the Home Secretary and Minister for Transport and also, 'a short report on one sheet of paper showing the numbers that could be accommodated on various [Underground] sections.'

On 22 September, the Sunday newspapers reflected just how far the tide had turned. The *Sunday Dispatch* reported that 30,000 people had slept in Tube stations the previous night and that, 'by 6 p.m. there seemed no vacant space from St Paul's to Notting Hill, from Hampstead to Leicester Square,' where, 'Settees were carried from the waiting hall … to accommodate children.' Already a pattern was emerging that people bombed out of their homes were effectively living in the stations and eating at friends' and relatives' homes during the day.[11] The *Sunday Express* described, 'Trains moving west were crowded with people carrying blankets, pillows and cases.'[12]

For *Reynold's News*, Montagu Slater (usually the newspaper's theatre critic) vividly described the cat-and-mouse behaviour of both staff and shelterers:

I reached the Angel station just as the nightly siren was moaning at 8.30. A policeman at the door was forbidding entrance to anyone with bedding, but the crowd surged past him. Inside the door there was an attempt to sort out the bona fide passengers from those who wanted shelter. When it was clear that this was impossible the station staff closed the booking office. An excited crowd pushed and scrambled round to the lifts. So the lifts were closed.[13]

Proving that nothing is new, the *Sunday Chronicle* complained:

Resentment has been expressed at the number of foreign refugees who, having no work to do, manage to grab the best places in the shelters.

A briefing note from around 24 September for the Minister of Information, Alfred Duff Cooper, recommended that the press should be strongly discouraged from reviving demands for deep shelters and off-the-record it was admitted that there simply were not enough building materials available to construct them and in particular there was a shortage of cement.[14] The latter had been a constant complaint from Haldane and the *Daily Worker*, with the blame being placed on a small number of large companies who had suppressed small producers and were effectively operating a cartel to restrict supply and control prices.

On Monday 23 September the War Cabinet met to discuss air raid shelter policy. It was noted that although the Aldwych branch could hold 2,500 people at most (other parts of the branch were being used by the British Museum to store exhibits, including the Elgin Marbles), there was, 'no other section of the Underground railway system, not required for traffic, which had not already been earmarked for some specific purpose.'[15] It was estimated that some 120,000 were sheltering in stations unofficially, which was manageable, but the situation would get worse as the nights drew in and darkness fell before the end of the evening rush-hour.

Writing for the *Daily Express* on Friday 27 September 1940, Sefton Delmer – the first British journalist to formally interview Adolf Hitler before his rise to power – put a positive spin on events, pointing out that unlike Londoners, German civilians:

> … can't go to the Berlin Underground. For in Berlin the underground is a shallow affair, only a few feet deep, because of the high level of surface water. It is not comparable for protection with the London Tube. Even if safety were the only consideration, I would rather take my bombing in London.

Around this time, Delmer was recruited by the Political Warfare Executive, later to produce some of the most notorious anti-Nazi 'black propaganda' of the war, including obscene doctored photographs of his former interviewee.

On the same day the *Daily Mirror* drew attention to the fact that while Archway station was packed with shelterers every night, trains were passing through empty platforms at the unfinished, but not yet opened Highgate. It was suggested that trains should stop to allow those who wished to shelter there to alight, 'even if the street entrances and exits are not complete.'[16] Meanwhile, the *Daily Worker* printed a letter from 'Some Underground Workers' reminding shelterers:

> People who shelter in the Tubes should realise that they are the guests, not of the LPTB, but of the employees of the station staff – stationmasters, foremen, ticket collectors, book clerks and porters. The board has not yet officially sanctioned the use of the stations as shelters and their instructions are still that the public are only allowed in the stations during raids on sufferance and that if the 'All Clear' sounds before the close of traffic, the stations are to be cleared of passengers and locked. We have seen that the staff have turned a blind eye and have completed ignored the Board's instructions and I think this fact should be fully apprehended by all of us as a splendid example of working-class solidarity.

On Thursday 3 October Admiral Sir Edward Evans, recently appointed London Regional Commissioner for Civil Defence, toured a number of Underground stations to assess the situation for himself. Reporters were assured that a ticketing system for shelterers would be introduced, the government was in favour of bunks being installed in stations and the deficiencies in sanitation would be addressed as soon as possible. In an interesting development, Admiral Evans justified the presence of some men in one shelter:

> The main thing is to ensure that working men are able to sleep in safe, healthy surroundings. We must not tolerate men who have worked all day being kept out of the shelters by people who have had all day to line up for the best places.[17]

Churchill's earlier request for details of which additional parts of the Underground could be used as shelters resulted in a reply, via the Minister for Home Security, on 9 October from Philip Allen, the private secretary to LPTB chairman Lord Ashfield. He indicated that four disused stations could provide substantial accommodation:

British Museum [closed 24 September 1933]:
    1,300 sq. ft. (subway)
    5,000 sq. ft. (platform tunnel)

City Road [closed 8 August 1922]:
    600 sq. ft. (subway to platforms)
    3,000 sq. ft. (platform tunnel)

South Kentish Town [closed 5 June 1924]:
    800 sq. ft. (subway to platforms)
    5,600 sq. ft. (platform tunnel)

York Road [closed 24 December 1932]:
    5,600 sq. ft. (platform tunnel)

British Museum could only be accessed from the running tunnels, while the others could be by that route, or from the street. In addition, other spaces in open stations were suggested, including the inverts under the island platforms at Angel (2,000 sq. ft), Clapham Common (900 sq. ft), Clapham North (1,000 sq. ft) and Euston (1,200 sq. ft) and various unused passageways at seven other stations (totalling 8,570 sq. ft). Allen stressed that all would still need to be properly assessed and made habitable.

Allen said that Lord Ashfield appreciated the need for food and drink to be provided to shelterers and that such a provision should be in the hands of a single authority, 'and that the service should not in any way be regarded as a commercial enterprise.' Progress had been made with first aid posts, which had already been established at ten stations across three boroughs:

Hampstead Borough Council:
  Belsize Park
  Chalk Farm
  Swiss Cottage

City Corporation:
  Bank
  St Paul's
  Moorgate

Kensington Borough Council:
  Holland Park
  Earls Court
  Gloucester Road
  South Kensington

On 22 October the War Cabinet met to discuss the progress that had been made up to 18 October. It was estimated that there had been 84,500 Tube shelterers on 20 September, reaching a peak of 120,000 on 25 September and since then it had fluctuated between 100,000 and 120,000 each night. The most pressing issue was sanitation, with local authorities having been ordered to take responsibility for the emptying and cleaning of the chemical toilets that the LPTB had installed, although this was still a temporary measure. The Board's engineers had devised a method of using the existing compressed air system at stations to force waste up to the level of the sewers, the total cost of which was estimated at £20,000 (£2.6 million today). Across the shelter network as a whole, it was said:

> No report of this nature would be complete without reference to the excellent behaviour of the public in the shelters. A few isolated instances have been brought to notice where people, usually the worse for drink, have made themselves a nuisance to others, but it cannot be too strongly emphasised that the behaviour of the shelterers as a whole has been orderly to the highest degree.[18]

With the authorities now resigned to public sheltering in the Underground, the Home Office requested that the Metropolitan Police Special Branch investigate conditions within the stations. On 31 October Inspector Arthur Cain reported that a questionnaire had been sent to the appropriate stationmasters, although they had not been told that it originated from Special Branch. The questions covered purely factual matters, such as the date the station was first used as a shelter, the average number of shelterers and so on, but also whether the staff were receiving the co-operation of the local authorities in housing them, as well as if there had been any 'incidents' of prostitution, hooliganism, drunkenness, political agitation, or interference with passengers attributed to shelterers.

Cain stated that on 23 October an estimated 132,000 people had sheltered in stations and on 27 October it was 129,000. Since each person paid at least 1½d (80p today) for a ticket allowing them to enter a station, the revenue to the LPTB from shelterers would be in the region of £825 per day (just over £100,000).

Although the stations had been used as shelters for about five weeks, only sixteen incidents were reported to the police and LPTB staff. These ranged from simple drunkenness, to a case of indecent assault. Communist activity was a major concern for the authorities, with six of the 'incidents' involving the distribution of seditious literature. It was reported that a self-appointed 'communist committee' was active at Belsize Park station, as well as the neighbouring Hampstead, but that both were actually composed of the same people, who were said not to represent the views of the majority of the shelterers at either station. The outlawed British Union of Fascists did not appear to be in evidence, but there had been some incidents of anti-semitism at Manor House station. This was attributed to the large number of Jewish shelterers, although the latter must have been true of a number of other stations without the same issues arising.

The chief practical problems were the clearance of litter and sanitation. Shelterers did not always tidy up after themselves when they left the stations. The provision of latrines was inadequate and stations with existing lavatories were being overwhelmed. Some local authorities seemed particularly reluctant to accept any responsibility for what would properly fall within their public health remit as regards stations in their areas. Although the individual questionnaires have not survived, the summarised results showed the conditions for sanitation and cleansing against the number of stations and average shelterers were:

Conditions	Sites	Shelterers
Adequate	9	14,350
Fair	56	99,050
Poor	14	23,900
Inadequate	3	9,100
Very Poor	1	4,000

There were some reports of LPTB employees accepting bribes (delicately described only as 'gratuities') for reserving shelter spaces and others of the unauthorised soliciting of money for staff collections. One was traced to maintenance (rather than station) personnel, but another was attributed to a porter at a station that did not actually employ one!

There were particular capacity problems at Piccadilly and Kentish Town stations due to the large number of troops passing through, many of whom ended up staying overnight, through lack of direction, in military hostels. Inevitably there had been cases of disorder, drunkenness and prostitution at Piccadilly Circus and hooliganism at Kentish Town. It

A plain-clothes detective and a London Transport official search a suitcase at the station left luggage office during the IRA bombing campaign.

Left: A special refreshments train being loaded. Right: Official warning against anti-social behaviour in the shelters. Note that spitting could incurr a substantial fine.

was suggested that one remedy would be the allocation of military police to deter such behaviour, although they could also direct service personnel to suitable accommodation elsewhere.

On the whole, shelterers were well-behaved, with card-playing and chess popular among the men, much knitting by the women and reading by all. Although there was a degree of romantic interaction between some of the adolescents, any 'hint of immorality' was strongly denied, but younger children could be troublesome due to natural restlessness. This manifested itself in playing along the platforms and passageways, but also in 'joy-riding' on trains between stations. It was suggested that some stations would benefit from having specifically segregated areas for mothers and children.

Reflecting the haphazard arrangements of the time, Shelter Marshals and First Aiders who wore armbands signifying their roles generally received better co-operation from shelterers than those without any such 'badge of office.' The majority of shelterers were content to accede to the guidance of the uniformed police officers on duty or LPTB staff. The Metropolitan Police's Women's Branch was noted as being particularly valued by the large percentage of female shelterers, who preferred not to rely on male officers in settling certain disputes.

Most LPTB staff similarly accepted their new responsibilities, but it was thought that others might benefit from specific guidance from management as to the scope of these duties. On 29 October the *Daily Express* had printed a letter from a reader in Oxford recounting a recent experience of using the Underground as a legitimate passenger:

There were only five of us in the lift and an elderly woman – about sixty-five, I should think – came to the lift with her bundle. She was barred by the attendant, who said: 'Shelter?' She said 'Yes.' He replied: 'You'll have to use the stairs.' He shut the gates with room for a good thirty people in the lift and the old woman had to go down all those stairs with her bundle. We were speechless with astonishment. Is the LPTB extending this sort of co-operation extensively?

On 25 October the *South London Press* reported a new 'racket' involving individuals – known as 'droppers' – gaining early admission to station shelters and then marking out multiple 'pitches' with blankets and clothing on behalf of shelterers who had paid them to do so. In some cases, the dropper would circumvent the queue by feigning medical reasons for not being able to stand in line. On 1 November the *Daily Express* reported that some droppers were 'reserving' up to twenty-five pitches at a time at the best stations, selling them on to desperate shelterers and making 'as much as £6 a night' – £800 today.

An only slightly more legitimate form of 'free enterprise' saw people living close to stations operating unofficial 'cloakrooms' for shelterers' bedding. The *Daily Mirror* reported that one flat-owner was accommodating the bedding of 400 people at a charge of 6d per week (£3.25 today), but hoped that, 'the owner of the flat sprays the 'cloakroom' regularly with some mild disinfectant and that the owner of each bundle takes it home occasionally to give it a good shaking and a thorough airing.'[19] Eventually these budding entrepreneurs were put out of business by the provision of cloakroom facilities in the stations themselves.

The introduction of bunks on platforms made better use of the available space, although the less lucky still had to sleep on the platform itself, as shown below.

Station cloakroom for storing the shelterers' bedding.

As the Blitz continued unabated, the conditions in the Tube shelters were gradually improved, most significantly with the provision of three-tiered bunks on platforms and in passageways, the first being installed at Lambeth [North] station on 25 November. Putting paid to the antics of the droppers, shelterers were allocated to numbered pitches and platforms were marked with two white lines: shelterers could occupy the space up to the first – eight feet from the platform edge – when they were admitted at 4 p.m. and after 7.30 up to the second line, four feet from the edge. The remainder was reserved for passengers, which no doubt raised some safety concerns, especially since one shelterer had already died after falling against a train at Shepherd's Bush station on 20 November.

Even before the advent of the bunks, a catering service for shelterers was introduced, commencing at Holland Park station on 29 October, and by 10 December it covered the entire open station shelter network. By mid-November, the Lord Mayor's Air Raid Distress Fund had raised £10,000 (approximately £1.3 million today) towards the cost of refreshments equipment, this sum being matched by the Ministry of Food. Special refreshments trains were introduced, ferrying tons of food and gallons of drink direct to the platforms every night.

One of the original chief objections to the use of Tube stations as shelters was the potential for the spread of disease and now the same concerns resurfaced. In a series of articles for the popular *Picture Post* magazine in November 1940, John Langdon-Davies warned of the immense risks that the still relatively uncontrolled and unmonitored mass of people were willingly exposing themselves to.

He was particularly concerned with those diseases that could be inoculated against, especially diphtheria, which even in peace time killed almost 400 children in London every year, but in the closed confines of a poorly-ventilated Tube station could spread like wildfire. Children who were susceptible could be immunised at the cost of 'a few pence,' but the UK authorities had shown a marked reluctance to do this. Langdon-Davies blamed this on, 'the anti-vaccinationists; that bullying minority who would shorten the expectation of life of our children.'

He also stressed the need for kitchens to cook hot food and sick bays at larger shelters: 'Sick bay it must be – not a first aid post. Its job is not to bandage cuts but to fight infectious disease.' Everything had to be done to keep people using the shelters, 'in a condition of maximum efficiency for fighting and destroying the disease germs which will come at us from every quarter while we are hiding from Nazi bombs.'

Much of what Langdon-Davies advocated had either already, but only just, been implemented or would be before the end of 1940. Facilities to disinfect shelterers' bedding were already in place; the first compressed-air sewage ejectors were installed at Manor House station on 1 December; and the first medical aid post opened at South Kensington station on 20 December. Eventually there were eighty-six such posts by 8 March 1941, having cost £12,950 (£1.7 million) to set up.

Tube shelter life inevitably progressed beyond mere survival from the bombs on the surface. Libraries and night school classes were started at some stations, films, shows and other entertainments at others, including concerts by the Entertainments National Service Association (ENSA). On one occasion, during an air raid, even the legendary Glen Miller and his band played an impromptu session in the Tube station near the theatre where they were appearing. More than one 'shelter newspaper' appeared to provide information and guidance to its particular station's guests.

Even so, certain nights spent in the Tube shelters were far from jolly occasions and some visitors were less welcome than others. On leave in late 1940, Flight Lieutenant Guy Gibson – later to command the famed Dambusters Raid, but at the time flying night-fighters – was on leave in London when he found himself stranded at a mainline station during a heavy air raid. Venturing down to the adjacent Underground platforms, he quickly realised that his RAF uniform was provoking an air of distinct hostility. Eventually a woman stood up and yelled at him: 'Why don't you get up there and fight those bastards?' The future hero of the Ruhr made a hasty strategic withdrawal and took his chances with the bombs in the streets above. The civilian population, he thought, 'were getting decidedly jumpy.'[20]

Conversely, just as the Tube shelterers had developed a certain attitude to the armed forces, so the antagonism towards some men in the stations was still evident, particularly by those who were voluntarily not seeking any form of shelter at all. One lively exchange of letters in the *Daily Mirror* saw an Auxiliary Fire Service worker at Battersea – identified only as 'Molly' – complain:

For the yellow specimens of so-called men, who crawl and burrow their way into the depths of London's Underground stations, I have nothing but hate and contempt. They

The pioneering Medical Aid Post which
was set up at South Kensington station

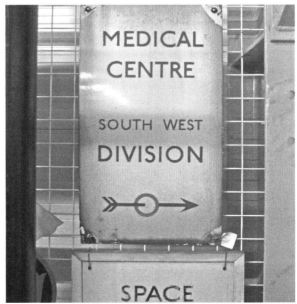

have no place among a magnificent generation that is putting up such a gigantic fight for its very existence and freedom ... No living soul likes the whistling of falling bombs, or the sight of blazing infernos, but to a MAN we look for a feeling of security. What security do these louts offer?[21]

This inevitably provoked an indignant response from shelterers at Belsize Park, who protested that they were working in war production, so needed to get a good night's sleep and demanded an apology. Such umbrage found little sympathy with the newspaper, which responded:

So you like your little beds, do you? Of course, it would be too much to expect that you volunteer for part-time Police, A.F.S., Home Guard, Spotter, Fire Watcher, Ambulance Driver, Rescue Worker, Stretcher Bearer or Warden's duties? To give up a LITTLE of your sleep, a FEW of your evenings is much too much to ask you![22]

Away from such ructions, progress was being made on converting some of the disused stations previously offered by the LPTB. South Kentish Town – on the Northern line, between Kentish Town and Camden Town – opened first. The original lift shaft was capped with concrete against bombs and dividing walls added between the former platform area and the track. Next was British Museum – just west of Holborn on the Central line – where the most was made of the available space by dividing the platform area into two levels, again walled off from the track. It opened to shelterers on 8 September 1941.

The last of the disused stations to be converted was City Road, between Old Street and

A children's party held at Holborn Station.

Angel, on the Northern line. Ove Arup, the Anglo-Danish philosopher and engineer who would later found the company that still bears his name, devised a plan to convert it to an air raid shelter, but his idea of splitting the platform area into two levels by using 6-inch thick pre-cast concrete floor slabs was initially rejected, even though the same feature had already been approved at British Museum. The station was not handed over to Finsbury Council for conversion until 1 September 1941, by which time the decision on the flooring was reversed, so it was constructed as planned.

On the Central line's eastern extension, the partially-completed Bethnal Green station and associated running tunnels eventually had bunks for 5,000 and could accommodate a further 5,000 (although it never went higher than 7,000 during the Blitz). This still made it the largest shelter maintained by Bethnal Green Borough Council, yet it had only one entrance, in addition to an emergency exit half a mile away in an adjoining borough. On 3 March 1943, it was the site of the largest British civilian loss of life during the war, when 173 people suffocated in a crush while attempting to enter the shelter during an air raid alert (see Chapter 6). Other sections of new Central line tunnels were used as public shelters by the West Ham Corporation and Leyton Borough Council.

The incomplete Highgate station was also adapted for shelterers in time to see some service before the end of the Blitz. The only disused or uncompleted station not to see some wartime function was York Road, on the long stretch between King's Cross and Caledonian Road on the Piccadilly line, presumably for the same reason it closed in the first place, i.e. it being in a largely industrial area, with little residential development nearby.

The Blitz ended on 21 May 1941, although the numbers of those sheltering in the stations fell only gradually. By July 1942 only 2,000 people were still staying overnight across the seventy-nine Tube station shelters, so it was decided to close around half of them on 1 August that year. Some still suffered psychologically from their experiences during the Blitz and were incapable of sleeping above ground (perhaps the only manifestation of the 'deep shelter mentality' so feared by the pre-war authorities), but for others, particularly those bombed out of their homes, life in the shelters was simply better overall. The *Daily Express* noted:

There are those who cannot afford to buy enough furniture for a new home; those who like the community night life of a shelter — the chatting, card-playing and singing, the canteens and the medical facilities.

One woman shelterer at Strand station explained:

I don't like living alone and find the company here pleasant. I've decided to move to Trafalgar-square, but don't expect to like it. They have such funny people there.

Most regular shelterers, it seems, were apt to think of anyone at any *other* shelter as being a bit 'odd.'

It was not until January 1944 that the *Luftwaffe* resumed its sporadic night attacks on London, but on such a small scale that it quickly acquired the sobriquet of the 'Baby Blitz.' It petered out at the end of May, with the vast majority of German aircraft used in the attacks having been destroyed. There was a respite of just fifteen days – punctuated by the British, American and Canadian invasion of Normandy on 6 June – before the first operational V-1 flying bomb was launched from France, eventually falling next to a railway bridge in Grove Road, Mile End.

Powered by a pulse-jet engine at a speed of 400 miles per hour, the V-1 carried rudimentary guidance equipment – designed to maintain a level course and then cut the engine by the time it was over the target area – and an 850 kg warhead. British intelligence had known Germany was developing unconventional weapons, but the appearance of the V-1 came as a complete surprise to a civilian population who thought their enemy's capacity to attack them had dwindled to nothing. It also took the military some time to develop the right combination of anti-aircraft guns, fighter aircraft and barrage balloons to bring down as many V-1s as possible, although inevitably many still got through. Those on the ground became all too familiar with the drone of the V-1's engine and the dread that when it stopped the impact was imminent.

While the V-1 could be at least be intercepted on a large scale, the same could not be said of the next of Hitler's *Vergeltungswaffen* – 'Revenge Weapons'. The V-2 ballistic missile was launched on a high parabolic track, reaching the edge of space, before falling back down to Earth in the general area of the target. Unless someone on the ground caught sight of the missile falling at terminal velocity, or heard and recognised the supersonic crack as it broke the sound barrier, the first, and possibly last, thing they knew would be impact and the 1,000 kg warhead exploding.

The first V-2 hit Chiswick on 8 September and the last Orpington, Kent, at 4.54 p.m. on 27 March 1945 (the penultimate landed in Stepney, East London, at 7.21 a.m. the same day), with not a single day between not seeing at least one launch at London, totalling 1,358 missiles in all. The only thing that spared the capital a greater assault was that an even higher number were aimed at the Belgian port of Antwerp – the main entry point for Allied troops and supplies at the time – as well as smaller numbers of other British and European cities.

The appearance of the V-weapons resulted in a resurgence in the numbers sheltering in the Tube network, which by then had been augmented with the deep level shelters first mooted in late 1940 (see next chapter). By the beginning of 1945, 25,000 people were still sheltering in the stations, but four months later it had dropped to a mere 8,000. With victory in Europe assured, the order to dismantle most of the bunks in the Tube shelters was issued and on 13 April the first of them were removed from Finsbury Park station. By noon a hundred had gone, with twenty left in place, 'just in case.'

As the encircling Soviet troops fought their way through the streets of Berlin, Adolf Hitler committed suicide in his bunker under the Reich Chancellery on 30 April and Germany surrendered unconditionally a week later. Back in London, catering services for Tube shelterers ceased on 3 May and on the last day of the month, at South Wimbledon, the last medical aid post and bunks on the open station network were removed.

Chapter 3 References:

1. Haldane, J. B. S., *Daily Worker*: 'The £.S.D. of Preventing This!' (London: 23 June 1938), p. 2.
2. *Daily Worker*: 'London Can Be Safe From Air Attack.' (London: 22 October 1938), p. 4.
3. This was only a month after the premiere of *Things to Come* – perhaps the reporter's mind had been focused having seen it?
4. HO 201/7.
5. Emmerson & Beard, pp. 60–61.
6. Clayton, 139.
7. London Transport Museum collection.
8. HO 207/503.
9. *The Times*: 'No Sheltering in the Tubes – Appeal to the Public.' (London: 19 October 1940), p. 4.
10. *The Times*: 'Aldwych Tube May be a Shelter.' (London: 21 October 1940), p. 2.
11. *Sunday Dispatch*: '30,000 Spent Last Night in Tubes.' (London: 22 October 1940).
12. *Sunday Express*: 'Tube sleepers 'stake claims' in afternoon.' (London: 22 October 1940).
13. *Reynold's News*: 'What shall we do about shelters?' (London: 22 October 1940).
14. HO 186/321.
15. CAB 21/773.
16. *Daily Mirror*: 'Underground Conundrum.' (London: 27 September 1940), p. 2.
17. *Daily Express*: 'Special Tickets For Underground Shelters Soon.' (London: 4 October 1940).
18. CAB 21/773.
19. *Daily Mirror*: 'Flat Rate.' (London: 2 December 1940), p. 4.
20. Gibson, 1946, Chapter X.
21. *Daily Mirror*: 'Shelter Rats!' (London: 1 January 1941), p. 5.
22. *Daily Mirror*: 'Shelter Rats (Contd.)' (London: 8 January 1941), p. 5.

Above left, the surviving fragment of the Brompton Road facade in Cottage Place. Right, the unassuming entrance to the disused Down Street station.

Anti-aircraft control room in the former lift shaft at the disused Brompton Road Station.

CHAPTER 4

DEEP DEFENCE

Parallel to the use of London Underground infrastructure for public sheltering – but largely unseen – was similar conversion for official purposes. Conspicuous in their absence from the 9 October 1940 letter from the LPTB to the Minister for Home Security (see last chapter) detailing additional parts of the Underground that might be available for civilian shelterers were two disused Piccadilly line stations.

The first of these was Brompton Road – between Knightsbridge and South Kensington – which closed on 29 July 1934. On 4 November 1938 His Majesty's Commissioners of Crown Lands paid £24,000 (£3.6 million today) on behalf of the War Office for the entirety of the station, including the surface buildings and lift shafts. As trains were still running through the platform tunnels, a shielding wall was built alongside the tracks and the area turned into office space. The two 23-foot diameter lift-shafts were suitably capped with reinforced concrete and one of them was turned into the four-storey operations centre for the 1st Anti-Aircraft Division, which was tasked with defence of the capital against enemy air attacks.

Situated down a quiet side street off Piccadilly and only a short distance from Green Park to the east and Hyde Park Corner to the west, Down Street station was so little used that it closed on 21 May 1932. In March 1939 it was decided that it would be an ideal location for the secure and protected headquarters for the Railway Executive Committee (REC), which had been created as a co-ordinating authority for all of Britain's railways – including the London Underground – during time of war.

As at Brompton Road, a wall had to be constructed between the former platform area and the tracks, but due to the heightened need for secrecy, at Down Street this had to be done covertly during non-traffic hours. About half the length of each platform tunnel was turned into dormitories and the rest was allocated to the kitchen, staff messes, electrical services, telephone exchange and a small number of offices. Small sections of platform were retained at the eastern (Green Park) end, which allowed visitors to surreptitiously arrive or leave via the driver's cabs of passing trains. A plunger-activated red signal was provided on each 'platform' to indicate that drivers should stop. One of the fortuitously long passageways from the platforms to the lifts was retained for ventilation purposes, while the other was divided into various offices, a committee room and the typists' room. An additional exit passageway was used for lavatories and bathrooms and a small two-person cigar-shaped passenger lift was run down the centre of the emergency spiral staircase.

Although intended solely for REC, during the first half of the Blitz, Down Street was also used by Churchill, as the Cabinet War Rooms in Whitehall had not yet been completed. He remembered it as a 'considerable underground office in Piccadilly... From the middle of October [1940] till the end of the year I used to go there once the firing had started, to transact my evening business and sleep undisturbed.'

Elsewhere the need for secure LPTB office accommodation was fulfilled by disused areas at Hyde Park Corner, Knightsbridge and South Kensington stations, while Leicester Square housed the central control room used to warn specific Underground stations of impending air attack, ahead of the main air raid siren system. At Green Park, disused areas of the original Dover Street station were utilised by the LPTB chairman and principal officers as an air raid shelter. The Aldwych branch platforms at Holborn were converted into wartime headquarters for the LPTB, comprising offices and dormitories.

Alongside the Piccadilly line platforms at Earl's Court were two 40-foot lengths of platform tunnel originally intended to form part of an 'express' District line between there and Mansion House. From 1927 to 1939 it was the home of the Underground's signalling school, but during the War, part of it housed recording equipment linked to hydrophones in the Thames, designed to detect the impact of delayed action bombs in the river bed that might threaten the Tube tunnels below (see Appendix 2). The South Kensington tunnels were also used as the LT Chief Engineer's emergency headquarters,[1] linked via the pedestrian tunnel under Exhibition Road to an ARP HQ under the Natural History and Geological Museums.

A similar adaptation to that at Brompton Road – but on a much larger scale – was carried out at the original St Paul's station building, which closed when superseded by escalators and a new ticket hall several hundred yards away on 1 January 1939. In October 1940 the site was leased to the Central Electricity Board, which turned the two former lift shafts – 23 feet in diameter and 120 feet deep – into the multi-levelled standby control centre for the nascent National Grid. The original emergency stairs were retained for access, while part of a ventilation shaft was used for storage. All four shafts were suitably capped with reinforced concrete, which proved an effective defence when the surface building was bombed in June 1941.

Apart from the civilian shelters described in the previous chapter, some of the unused Central line eastern extension tunnels also found a more covert use. A section of tunnel between Wanstead and Gant's Hill stations became an underground factory for the Plessey Company, making military electronic components including wiring sets for Halifax and Lancaster bombers, wireless equipment, field telephones and electro-mechanical 'Bombes' for the Enigma code-breakers at Bletchley Park. Access was via the unfinished Wanstead, Redbridge and Gant's Hill stations, as well as temporary lift-shafts installed at Cambridge Park and Danehurst Gardens. Work began in late 1940 and was completed by March 1942, with some of the spoil from the central London Deep Shelters (see below) used

The Plessey factory in the Central Line tunnels and, below, the part-time factory in the Earl's Court subway.

to increase the ground cover above the tunnels near Redbridge. The complex eventually comprised 300,000 square feet of floor-space, served by 2,000 workers and a narrow-gauge electric railway.

Another wartime factory was located in the long subway connecting the Piccadilly line platforms at Earl's Court station to the nearby exhibition centre.[2] From June 1942 until the end of the War, aircraft components were made by volunteer London Transport workers in their spare time. This was a satellite factory to the main centre of the London Aircraft Production Group (LAPG) at Chiswick bus garage, where Handley Page Halifax heavy bombers were built, beginning in late 1940. When the LPTB's remit for aircraft production was expanded, it was decided to use the partially-completed Northern line extension depot at Bushey Heath/Aldenham, where production began in October 1941. The first LAPG Halifax flew the following month and the LAPG built 710 in all. The aircraft company De Havilland and the engine-makers Napier also used the Aldenham site.

The Underground's Acton Works fulfilled a number of wartime roles. It built specialist breakdown lorries for the American army, made and tested bridging pontoons (LT staff also built the testing tank!) and over-hauled landing craft for the Admiralty. In the run-up to D-Day, it worked on converting existing tanks into the specialist armoured assault vehicles devised by Major General Percy Hobart – known as 'Hobart's Funnies' – including bridge-layers and amphibious Duplex Drive Shermans. The signals department even made the bomb-detecting hydrophones mentioned above.

After the bombing of mid/late 1940, in the October of that year, it was decided to build a number of large deep level shelters of the type championed in certain quarters, although nothing like on the scale demanded by some. An early idea was to utilise lift shafts rendered redundant by the installation of escalators at some stations, or the closure of others, by driving tunnels out from low level like the spokes of a wheel. The obvious drawbacks were the vulnerable single central entry point and that the shelter tunnels would not be much use for anything else after the War.

A revised plan envisaged a pair of parallel 1,400-foot long tube tunnels adjacent to or between the following Tube stations:

Northern line:
  Belsize Park
  Camden Town[3]
  Goodge Street
  Oval
  Stockwell
  Clapham North
  Clapham Common
  Clapham South
Central line:
  Chancery Lane
  St Paul's
  Liverpool Street & Bethnal Green (mid-point)

US Army breakdown lorry built at the Acton Works.

Testing a pontoon bridge at Acton.

Halifax bomber built by the London Aircraft Production Group.

Above: Sherman tanks arrive at Acton by rail for amphibious conversion.

Belsize Park south entrance.

Belsize Park south entrance.

Although all were connected to their Tube station proper, access was normally via separate double spiral staircases, which also had a small passenger lift running down the centre. In order to avoid a repetition of the devastating effects of the direct hits at Trafalgar Square, Balham and Bank stations (see next two chapters), the heads of the staircases were protected by massive squat drum-shaped blockhouses.

Construction of the first ten shelters began on 7 November 1940, but in mid-1941 it was decided that no more would be built. Oval, St Paul's and Liverpool Street/Bethnal Green were abandoned at fairly early stages, but the rest were completed by 1942 and subsequently enjoyed a variety of uses. Each shelter was built to hold approximately 8,000 people at a cost of £35–£42 (£4,250–£5,100) per person, although the original estimate was 9,600 at £15 per head. The shelters were divided up into different sections, each named after a famous historical figure to make it easier for the users to find their way around.

Although locations were never mentioned, the actual existence of the shelters was hardly secret, with many newspapers reporting their completion and *The Engineer* providing this detailed description in its issue of 18 September 1942:

> The tunnel shelters, completed in 1942, are all similar. Each lies directly beneath its Underground station ... Each shelter consisted of two parallel, 1,200-foot tunnels, divided into an upper and lower floor and furnished with iron bunks. There were extensions at right angles for first-aid posts, wardens' rooms, ventilation equipment and lavatories – which posed a particular problem, since the shelters were below the level of the sewage system.
>
> At each shelter, eight lavatory tunnels were driven 12 feet in diameter. Closets are of the Elsan type. At the far end of each lavatory a hopper has been installed into which closets are emptied. To keep out bottles, boots, clothing etc. all of which have been found to give trouble in other shelters, it was necessary to install a wire screen. The hoppers are connected by piping to a closed ejector placed in the bottom of the staircase shafts and the contents of the ejector periodically forced out by means of compressed air through a rising main, 6 in. diameter, up to sewer level in the street above.

It is well known that the idea was to link up the shelters to form 'express' tube lines after the war, although this was obviously not eventually done. At 16 feet 6 inches in diameter, the shelter tunnels were too small for platforms, so clearly the locations chosen would have been the stations missed out.

Bunks in the lower deck of a deep level shelter

Similar accommodation in the upper deck.

Connecting passageway in a Deep Level Shelter. Below, the kitchen facilities.

Deep Level Shelter Locations

Belsize Park (Northern line)
North entrance: Behind shops alongside 210 Haverstock Hill
South entrance: Corner of Haverstock Hill and Downside Crescent
Used as a public shelter from 23 July to 21 October 1944, then closed due to low usage (shelterers transferred to Camden Town). The shelter sections were named after famous explorers (e.g. Livingstone, Rhodes, etc.).

Camden Town (Northern line)
North entrance: Buck Street, behind station
South entrance: Stanmore Place, Underhill Street[4]
Used as a hostel for Commonwealth troops from September 1943, until being made available as a public shelter from 16 July 1944 to 7 May 1945. The shelter sections were named after famous generals (e.g. Kitchener, Wellington, etc.).

Chancery Lane (Central line)
North entrance: 31-33 High Holborn
East entrance: Furnival Street
South entrance: Tooks Court[5]
Used as a troop hostel from 28 November 1942, as a hostel for female service personnel transferred from Goodge Street from 3 January 1944 and by the research & development branch of the Special Operations Executive from early 1944. The shelter sections were named after famous political leaders (e.g. Cromwell, Disraeli, etc.).

Clapham Common (Northern line)
North entrance: Corner of Clapham High Street and Carpenter's Place
South entrance: Corner of Clapham High Street and Clapham Park Road
Used as a hostel for American troops during 1943 and as accommodation for key government workers from June 1944. The shelter sections were named after famous engineers (e.g. Brunel, Stephenson, etc.).

Clapham North (Northern line)
North entrance: 400 Clapham High Road
South entrance: In yard behind station
Used as a hostel for male National Fire Service (NFS) personnel from 12 May 1943, until being made available as a public shelter from 13 July to 21 October 1944, when closed due to low usage (shelterers transferred to Clapham South). The shelter sections were named after famous writers (e.g. Dickens, Shakespeare, etc.).

Clapham South (Northern line)
North entrance: On Clapham Common, corner of The Avenue and Clapham Common South Side
South entrance: 4/6 Balham Hill

Used as weekend leave accommodation for British troops from 1943, until being made available as a public shelter from 19 July 1944 to 7 May 1945, although the Northern section and entrance had been closed since 21 October 1944. The shelter sections were named after famous naval commanders (e.g. Drake, Nelson, etc.).

Goodge Street (Northern line)

North entrance: Tottenham Court Road, opposite Torrington Place
South entrance: Chenies Street
Parts used by British and American forces – included General Dwight Eisenhower's London headquarters – from 31 March 1943 and as a hostel for female NFS personnel from 12 May 1943. Closed completely on 3 January 1944 when all users transferred to Chancery Lane. The shelter sections were named after famous scientists (e.g. Faraday, Newton, etc.).

Stockwell (Northern line)

North entrance: Traffic island, junction of Clapham Road and South Lambeth Road
South entrance: Studley Road
Used as a weekend hostel for British troops from 23 January 1943, then accommodation for American troops from September 1943. Made available as a public shelter from 9 July 1944 to 7 May 1945, although the Southern section and entrance has been closed from 21 October 1944. The shelter sections were named after famous artists or architects (e.g. Constable, Wren, etc.).

Chapter 4 References:
1.   MT 6/2759.
2.   This subway – which has an original 1930s escalator shaft at one end – is still little-used and so remains a popular location for film and television production.
3.   These first two replaced early considerations of Mornington Crescent and Warren Street; Leicester Square was similarly ruled out at an early stage.
4.   Next to Marks & Spencer car park.
5.   A 1980s addition.

Camden Town north entrance and, below, the south entrance

The Goodge Street north entrance.

Goodge Street south entrance. This is the only one to feature the secondary hexagonal structure on the right. The memorial commemorates 12 Bn. London Regiment in the First World War.

Clapham North south entrance. Clapham Common north entrance is shown below.

The Stockwell north entrance has been painted as a war memorial by local school children. Below, Stockwell south entrance.

Clapham south entrance, now incorporated into a new residential development. A plaque near the entrance explains the significance of this structure and the scale of the underground shelter.

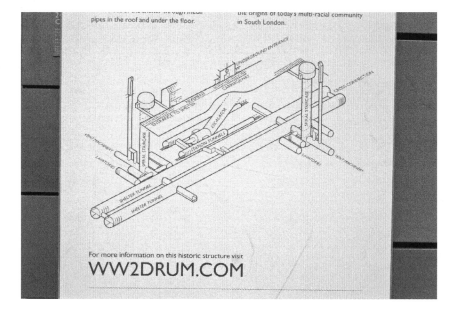

Clapham North north entrance – still looking for new occupiers.

Belsize Park north entrance.

Opposite, Belsize Park south entrance.

Clapham Common, rear of north entrance. Below, Clapham South north entrance when completed.

Clapham South north entrance, with the same view today as shown in the lower photograph opposite, but shorn of its ventilation ducts.

Clapham Common south entrance.

CHAPTER 5

THE BLITZ AND BEYOND

Complete details of all known war damage to the Underground would fill this book several times over; what follows are some of the most significant or destructive incidents.

The Blitz

7–8 September 1940

On the afternoon of 7 September, 364 Luftwaffe bombers – escorted by 515 fighters – targeted the area of the docks, although many bombs fell on surrounding residential areas. As evening fell, a second wave of 133 bombers attacked. In total 436 people were killed and 1,666 injured. The Ministry of Home Security's Damage Appreciation the following morning stated:

> Practically the whole of the enemy effort during the last twenty-four hours was devoted to the attack on LONDON, with an acute concentration of the DOCK AREAS, RAILWAYS and POWER STATIONS.[1]

Approximately twenty-four railway stations were hit in the south and east of the capital, including those on the London Underground network. At around 7 p.m., Blackfriars station was hit by a High Explosive (HE) bomb, knocking out the signalling and leaving traffic, 'practically at a standstill.'[2]

The joint LPTB/Southern Railway New Cross Gate station was hit by five HEs, injuring two SR workers,[3] one of whom died in hospital the following day. A five year old boy was killed at East Ham station on the District line (see Appendix 1).

There was minor damage at the Northern line Elephant & Castle station,[4] but at Plaistow on the District line, one car of a train standing at the station was blown on top of another. The wreckage was cut up on site and through-service resumed within twenty-four hours.[5]

11 September 1940

Wapping station burnt out by Incendiary Bombs (IB).[6,7]

19 September 1940
A bomb through the tunnel roof at Euston Square station at 1.20 a.m. killed two permanent way men (see Appendix 1) and flying glass injured passengers on a train. [8, 9]

25 September 1940
HE damaged Colindale station – close to RAF Hendon – at 8.45 p.m.,[10] and a number of passengers on a recently-arrived train were injured by flying glass.[11] At 11.45 p.m. a second HE completely demolished the station, injuring a number of staff, passengers and rescue workers,[12] eight of them fatally (see Appendix 1).

6 October 1940
HE outside Tooting Broadway station burst a 30-inch water main, but the flood-gates in the station prevented inundation.[13, 14]

8 October 1940
At 8.50 a.m. a HE penetrated the roof of Charing Cross (now Embankment) station and exploded on the District line track. Although there was no damage to the river wall or an adjacent water main, the ticket hall was wrecked, killing one person (see Appendix 1) and injuring nineteen more. Station closed.[15, 16]

12 October 1940
At 8.52 a.m. a bomb hit the Bakerloo line's Trafalgar Square (now Charing Cross) station, killing seven people (see Appendix 1). See next chapter for further details.

Extensive damage to sub-surface line in cutting.

Temporary repairs to bomb damage on the night of 15–16 September 1940 to the viaduct at Kilburn station are put to the ultimate test.

13 October 1940

A bomb close to Stanmore station at 8.07 a.m. injured a booking clerk and killed one person living in the flats above the station (see Appendix 1). Glass in the station was smashed and LPTB huts damaged.[17]

At 9.15 p.m. a bomb demolished two houses next to Bounds Green station, causing the collapse of the east end of the westbound platform tunnel, killing or mortally wounding seventeen people (see Appendix 1). See next chapter for further details.

Paddington (Praed Street) station on the Metropolitan line was hit by three bombs at 11 p.m., damaging the roof, platforms and track.[18] Eight people were killed or died later (see Appendix 1).

14 October 1940

At 8.02 p.m., a 1,400 kg 'Esau' semi-armour piercing bomb caused the collapse of the north end of the northbound platform tunnel at Balham station, resulting in multiple fatalities (see Appendix 1). See next chapter for further details.

At 8.57 p.m. a 250 kg bomb exploded on the west side of Camden Town station, demolishing part of the building and damaging and blocking the top of the escalators. At the time a number of people were sheltering from the air raid, both on the platforms and at the top of the escalators, and five were killed immediately or died later (see Appendix 1). Approximately fifteen members of the public and five LPTB staff were injured. As only the station building was damaged, traffic through this vital choke-point on the Northern line was not significantly interrupted.[19, 20, 21, 22, 23, 24]

A 500 kg bomb exploded over the Piccadilly line about 100 yards south of Holloway Road station at 9.30 p.m. It was later discovered that segments of both tunnels were cracked, partially filling them with clay for about 60 feet. Low tension cables were burnt through and the current rail was displaced for, 'a considerable length,' although there was reported to be little ingress of water. Repairs were started on 18 October and finished on 3 December, with traffic resuming two days later.[25, 26, 27, 28]

Damage to sub-surface line.

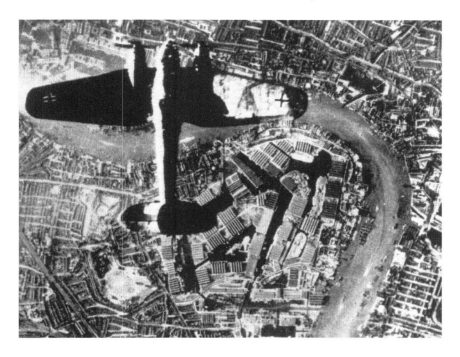

A Heinkel He 111 bomber flies north over the Surrey Commercial Docks, almost exactly along the track of the East London line between Rotherhithe and Shadwell.

16 October 1940

At 3.44 a.m. a HE breached the Metropolitan line tunnels between King's Cross and Farringdon Street stations, rupturing both gas mains and the Fleet sewer and filling the tunnels with gas and flooding water. Two patrolmen were trapped and one man was killed at Farringdon Street station (see Appendix 1). At 3.52 two DAs were reported at Aldersgate (now Barbican) station. Power to tracks and lighting failed. [29, 30]

The Metropolitan line platforms at King's Cross were hit at 8.05, breaking windows in a linesmen's hut and scattering debris on the track.[31] The damage was so severe that the platforms were re-sited some 275 yards to the east, coming into service on 14 March 1941.[32]

20 October 1940

Bomb damage at the Waterloo & City depot at Waterloo blocked two sidings with debris, which took three days to clear.[33]

Kensington (Addison Road) station was hit by multiple HEs at 8.50 p.m., various station buildings being partly or wholly destroyed and the track cratered and damaged.[34] This station was the terminus of a short Metropolitan line branch south-west of Latimer Road, with Uxbridge Road as the only intermediate station. Uxbridge Road had been hit by an HE on the night of 25–26 September and the branch had thus been closed between then and 3 October already. There was no attempt to reinstate the branch after the Kensington

[Addison Road] bombing, but the latter was reopened as Kensington [Olympia] after the War, the terminus of the short District line branch to serve the exhibition centre. The new Overground Shepherd's Bush station is partially built on the Uxbridge Road site.

21 October 1940

At 10.16 p.m., HE severely damaged the tunnels between Mornington Crescent and Euston on the Charing Cross branch of the Northern line. See next chapter for further details.

9 November 1940

Some flooding of the Waterloo & City line due to bomb damage.[35]

12 November 1940

Direct hit on Sloane Square station by large calibre bomb at 9.50 p.m., causing extensive damage and multiple casualties (see Appendix 1). See next chapter for further details.

At 10.35 p.m. three High Explosive bombs hit Wood Lane [White City] station on the Hammersmith & City line,[36] partly demolishing one viaduct arch and a platform. Gas mains were also broken.[37, 38]

15–16 November 1940

During the night a HE struck the recently disused[39] Metropolitan line Lord's station, mid-way between Baker Street and St John's Wood (Bakerloo). When the station was reconstructed in the mid-1920s, a mezzanine garage had been built over the tracks and the explosion scattered cars and other debris on the line. The High-Tension feeder was damaged, but no casualties were reported.[40, 41]

At 3.10 a.m. on 16 November, a 500 kg bomb in the car park at Arnos Grove broke glass in the station[42] and a fractured water main caused partial flooding of platform and track area.[43]

8 December 1940

A 1,000 kg HE hit the road outside Waterloo mainline station, opposite the Great War Victory Arch, causing a 70-foot diameter crater and breaching the Waterloo & City line tunnels, which were in cut-and-cover at this point. Water from fractured mains flowed down into the tunnels, flooding them completely. Repair work took more than three months.[44]

29–30 December 1940

After a lull in the bombing raid over Christmas, the Luftwaffe returned with a vengeance on the evening of 29 December.

At Moorgate IBs on the roof of the sub-station at 7.25 p.m. burnt it out completely. At midnight the station itself was evacuated due to the possibility of collapse of buildings backing onto the track.[45] A train standing at the station was partially destroyed. The undamaged half of one Q Stock trailer was later 'cut-and-shut' with a similar half of a P Stock motor car previously damaged at Plaistow on 7 September to create the unique 'new' motor car 14233. [46, 47]

Above: Fire damage to the station at Moorgate.

The two damaged halves of rolling stock being joined together.

Lambeth North station today – the buildings on the right are on the site of the bomb-demolished hostel

The South Kentish Town station today.

5 January 1941
At 9.01 a.m., a HE damaged the original Bakerloo line Waterloo station building on York Road, injuring one person. Another HE at 9.36 blocked the main LPTB ticket hall, although this was cleared before the commencement of traffic the next day.[48, 49] One person was mortally wounded at Turnpike Lane station, details unknown (see Appendix 1).

11 January 1941
Direct hit on the Central line ticket hall at Bank station, killing or mortally wounding over fifty people (see Appendix 1) and seriously injuring sixty-nine, as well as damaging trains at the platforms and causing a 120-foot crater across the road junction. See next chapter for further details. HE landed in the road between the entrances to Green Park station at 8.18 p.m., damaging both of them (the north one seriously) and the ticket hall,[50, 51] and killing a number of people (see Appendix 1).

16 January 1941
At 3.56 a.m. a huge SC 1,800 kg fragmentation bomb struck a hostel at 92 Westminster Bridge Road, near Lambeth (North) station. As well as killing a large number of people in the hostel, the explosion caused extensive damage to part of the northbound platform tunnel and slight damage to the southbound one, as well as the single track tunnel leading to the nearby London Road Depot and minor damage to the Northern line tunnels deeper down. The station roof was also damaged.[52, 53] Twenty people in the station were injured, with one dying in hospital two weeks later (see Appendix 1).

9 March 1941
Two HEs struck the sub-surface Metropolitan line King's Cross station at 11.45 p.m. A signal box was burnt out, superficial damage caused to the booking office and station building and the track blocked with debris.[54] One person killed (see Appendix 1).

19 March 1941
A bomb on the line at Whitechapel station at 9.30 p.m. damaged the tracks, a train, a sub-station and the station building.[55]

16–17 April 1941
Slight damage to Chalk Farm station over night due to a HE – services not disrupted;[56] one person killed (see Appendix 1). There was also HE damage to the Bakerloo line Elephant & Castle station, causing suspension of traffic.[57] Loss of current to the Waterloo & City line prevented services running on the morning of 17 April.[58]

19 April 1941
Royal Navy mine-sweeping operations in the Thames closed the Waterloo & City line on a precautionary basis.[59] A 500 kg bomb to the west of Arnos Grove station caused slight damage and disruption of service between there and Enfield West (now Oakwood).[60] The former St Mary's station – in use as a public shelter – was bombed, killing six people (see Appendix 1).

10–11 May 1941

This night saw particularly heavy raids, causing widespread damage to the Underground. At 12.10 a.m. a bomb hit the headquarters at 55 Broadway, while another went through the District line tunnels between St James's Park and Victoria, damaging cables. At 12.55 a train was damaged by blast near Victoria, as was a Circle line train at King's Cross five minutes later. The Bakerloo line's London Road depot was hit at 1.30, with five trains damaged. There was further hits at Aldgate (1.35), Rotherhithe (1.46), Paddington (Hammersmith & City (1.46) and Baker Street (1.57), where one electric and one steam train were damaged.

A bomb in the tunnel between Victoria and Sloane Square blocked the track and damaged cables (1.54); the platform was cracked at Tufnell Park (2.02); Great Portland Street was badly damaged (2.02); and Drayton Park was damaged by blast (2.50).

As fire raged around the Elephant & Castle, the stationmaster collected five colleagues and appealed to the shelterers on the platforms for assistance. Astonishingly, out of the thousands present, only one shelter warden and a sixty year-old man volunteered. The stationmaster, his colleagues and the two volunteers valiantly fought the fire, despite a minimum of equipment and no hoses, as bombs had fractured the water mains in the street. After successfully holding back the flames, when the All Clear sounded in the morning, the stationmaster watched the shelterers leaving, recalling later:

> Even now I can see the look of amazement on their faces as they made their way out of the station and saw the amount of destruction that had taken place during the night, whilst they been down below safe and sound ...[61]

Remarkably, in this night of such devastation, in which some 1,400 people were killed in London, the only ones on LU property were two Air Raid Wardens at Chalk Farm station (see Appendix 1).

The Blitz proper ended ten days later, yet the damage caused by the raids of 10–11 May resulted in disruption lasting for much longer, as not all could be repaired quickly – nor all the unexploded bombs cleared – at least not until after it was clear the main assault had finished.

Beyond the Blitz

At 1.53 a.m. on 6 June 1941, a stick of five HEs straddled Acton Works and Acton Town station, causing extensive damage to the Lifting Shop, the Smith's Shop and No. 1 & 3 roads. The Acton Town signal box and the sub-station were also damaged.[62]

Over the next eighteen months, the main disruptions to the Underground were more mundane, with storm damage on 12 July, fused cables at Acton Town on 27 July and the District line Charing Cross (now Embankment) on 3 September,[63] and a derailment at Parson's Green on 15 May 1942.[64]

In late 1941, the Luftwaffe had begun experimenting with the new tactic of equipping fast Messerschmitt Bf 109 fighters with a small bomb load and using them for fast 'tip-and-run' raids. In this configuration the aircraft were designated as *Jagdbombers* – 'pursuit bombers.' The raids were largely concentrated on shipping in the English Channel, or coastal land targets. In mid-1942, they switched to the new Focke-Wulf Fw 190, which could carry a single fuselage-mounted 500 kg bomb and two additional 50 kgs under each wing. Around noon on 20 January 1943, twenty-eight *Jagdbombers* attacked the London docks area. The East London line Surrey Docks (now Surrey Quays) overground station was machine-gunned, damaging the roof of the electricity sub-station.[65, 66]

A particularly heavy raid on 3 March resulted in an HE causing a 30-foot crater at the Brent Sidings, Willesden, while an unexploded bomb suspended services between Northwick Park and Preston Road stations. Falling anti-aircraft shells damaged Poplar and West Ham stations.[67]

Even though air raids were rare by this stage of the war, many people were still sheltering in Tube stations. On 15 March, Waterloo station had to be closed to shelterers due to issues with the ability to clear the platforms in the event of flood-gate damage.[68]

The Baby Blitz

The resumption of sustained night-time bombing in early 1944 was on such a smaller scale than the Blitz of 1940–1941 that there was little significant damage to the Underground until the night of 18–19 February. A phosphorous IB pierced the Metropolitan line tunnel near Queens Terrace, Finchley Road, and at 1.10 a.m., a HE at Goldhawk Road demolished a footbridge and blocked the line. At 1.17, the bridge carrying the Central line over Old Oak Common at the junction with Brunel Road was demolished. An unexploded bomb at South Wimbledon suspended services between Tooting Broadway and Morden.[69]

On 20 February IBs penetrated the lift shafts at Gloucester Road station,[70] then there was a respite until the early hours of the 23rd. At 12.32 a.m., an unexploded bomb was reported at Latimer Road station, then at 12.45, a HE caused damage to the viaduct and closed the station. At 12.40, a HE at Hounslow East damaged the Piccadilly line tracks and the sub-station. IBs caused fires at both the Metropolitan and Central line Shepherd's Bush stations at 12.44.[71] A HE at Alperton at 2.55 on 2 March closed the Piccadilly line between Acton Town and South Hounslow for ten-and-a-half hours.[72]

Cutaway of the V-1 Flying Bomb. They were known variously as 'Buzz-Bombs' and 'Doodlebugs' because of the distinctive sound of their Argus pulsejet engines. *(JC)*

V-1 launch ramp in northern France. *(CMcC)*

The V-Weapons Assault

The nature of the only superficially-guided V-Weapons resulted in sporadic damage to the Underground, mostly from V-1 Flying Bombs. The first was blast damage at 9.30 a.m. on 18 June to Essex Road station on the Northern City line, resulting in its closure and the introduction of a replacement bus service.

At 11.22 on 23 June a V-1 damaged the tracks and the viaduct beneath between Ravenscourt Park and Hammersmith. Temporary repairs allowed the resumption of eastbound services at 8.45 a.m. the next day and westbound services at 9.20, both with a 5 mph speed restriction, which lasted until 10.28 a.m. on the 28th.

A V-1 damaged a railway bridge and cables east of Hounslow East at 8.15 p.m. on 30 June and another four days later blocked all lines out of Wimbledon station, superficially damaging the LPTB sub-station.[73]

There was a direct hit by a V-1 on the East London line tracks between Shoreditch and News Cross at 4.57 p.m. on 12 July, while another at 5.03 a.m. on 17 July closed Walham Green (now Fulham Broadway) station, suspending District line services. At 4.40 a.m. the next day, there was a hit at New Cross station, although only the Southern Railway tracks were affected. Charing Cross mainline station was hit on 28 July at 9.48 p.m., with superficial blast damage caused to the LPTB station (now Embankment). At 11.10 p.m. the next day, a hit at West Brompton suspended services for two days.

Surrey Docks station was out of action for a day after a hit on 13 August, while Kensal Green station was severely damaged at 12.47 p.m. on 21 August. The District line tunnel was damaged and flooded at the junction of Bute Street and Harrington Street, South Kensington, at 3.45 a.m. on 22 August.

Considering its location so far away from central London, the V-1 that hit Aldenham Depot on 14 December must have been a complete fluke. It caused slight structural damage to the part of the facility being used by the Napier engine-maker.[74] At 7.12 a.m. on 13 January 1945, a District line train was damaged by blast at Bow.[75]

There are only three known instances of V-2 damage to the Underground. The first, on 22 January 1945, caused blast damage to Borough station, closing it to shelterers for the next two nights. The other two damaged Hyde Park Corner and Goodge Street stations on 18 and 25 March respectively. The V-2 assault ended two days later.[76]

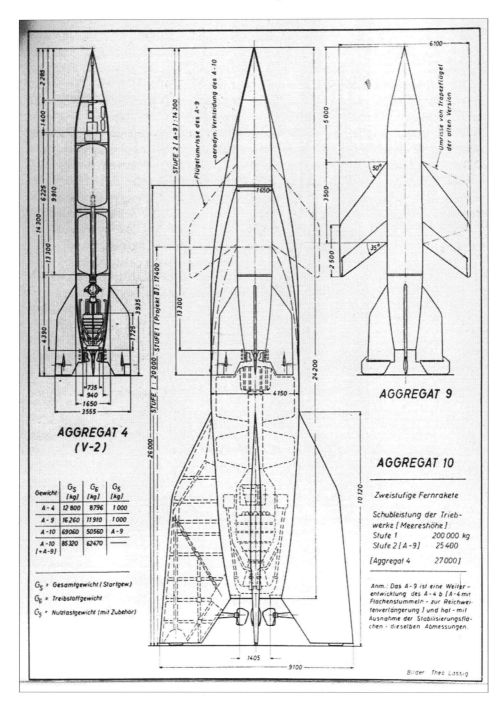

Diagram of Germany's proposed family of ballistic rockets. Only the V-2, on the left and known by them as the A4, was deployed.

Chapter 5 References:

1. HO 201/2.
2. HO 201/2.
3. Brooksbank, p. 14.
4. Horne & Bayman, p. 56.
3. Connor, Piers, p. 58.
4. Leboff, p. 145.
5. Day & Reed, p. 146.
6. AN 2/1104.
7. HO 192/8.
9. HO 201/2.
11. Horne & Bayman, p. 54.
12. AN 2/1104
13. AN 2/1105.
14. Horne & Bayman, p. 54.
15. AN 2/1105.
16. HO 201/3.
17. AN 2/1105.
18. AN 2/1105.
19. AN 2/1105.
20. HO 186/2419.
21. HO 192/8.
22. HO 201/3.
23. MT 6/2759.
24. MT 6/2766.
25. AN 2/1105.
26. HO 192/8.
27. MT 6/2759.
28. MT 6/2766.
29. AN 2/1105.
30. HO 201/3.
31. AN 2/1105.
32. Leboff, p. 81.
33. Gilham, p. 267.
34. Ministry of Home Security, Key Points Intelligence Directorate: Reports and Papers, Daily Reports – October 1940: Damage Appreciation 20-21/10/40, page 2 (Kew: National Archives, reference HO 201/3).
35. Gilham, p. 267.
36. The old station lay just to the south of the new Wood Lane station that opened in 2008.
37. AN 2/1106.
38. HO 201/4.
39. Last served 19 November 1939, after which Metropolitan lines services between Baker Street and Finchley Road – and between Finchley Road and Wembley – were superseded by new Bakerloo line stations on the same route.
40. AN 2/1106.
41. HO 201/4.
42. AN 2/1106.
43. Carpenter, p. 28.
44. Gilham, p. 267.
45. AN 2/1106
46. Day & Reed, pp. 146–147.
47. Now preserved by the Buckinghamshire Railway Society
48. AN 2/1107.
49. Gilham, p. 267.
50. AN 2/1107.
51. HO 201/6.
52. AN 2/1107.
53. HO 201/6.
54. HO 201/7
55. AN 2/1108.
56. HO 201/8
57. HO 201/8.
58. Gilham, p. 268.
59. Gilham, p. 268.
60. Carpenter, p. 28.
61. Graves, p. 78.
62. AN 2/1109.
63. AN 2/1110.
64. HO 201/10.
65. Goss, p. 50–55.
66. HO 201/14
67. HO 201/14.
68. Gregg, p. 89.
69. HO 201/16.
70. Croome, p. 54.
71. HO 201/16.
72. HO 201/16.
73. HO 201/16.
74. HO 201/17.
75. HO 201/18.
76. Gregg, p. 89.

An iconic view from the Blitz, showing the damage at Balham station where a bus has fallen into the bomb crater. See page 107 for more images from this event.

CHAPTER 6

MAJOR INCIDENTS

Trafalgar Square Station – 12 October 1940

At 8.52 p.m., a bomb hit the road directly over the Bakerloo line's Trafalgar Square (now Charing Cross) station and exploded on the escalator,[1] killing seven people (see Appendix 1).

At 10 a.m. on 13 October, Lt. Col. A. H. L. Mount, the Chief Inspecting Officer of Railways at the Ministry of Transport, visited the site and subsequently reported:

> At about 9 p.m. on 12/10, a bomb (presumably 250 kilo) fell on the roadway, making a shallow crater some 40 feet in diameter, which fractured water-mains and damaged some fourteen or fifteen rings of the 27-foot lower escalator chamber, the top of which is 42 feet below the surface. The soffit segments of three rings fell in, leaving a void above in the loose clay of the bomb crater. The dividing wall between the passages leading out of the escalator chamber was severely shattered and the outer wall damaged, leaving the roof joist dangerously supported. The lower headwall at the junction of the inclined tunnel and the lower chamber was also severely damaged.
>
> Small water-mains on the surface were fractured, but supply had been cut off. Water, however, was coming in at the top of the escalator.
>
> I was informed that of the people sheltering at the bottom of the escalator, ten were killed, ten seriously injured and ten less seriously injured.
>
> The running tunnels were not apparently affected, but a speed restriction was imposed, pending further examination.[2]

Contractors had already begun work and by the time of Mount's visit, scaffolding had been erected and necessary equipment put into place. Unfortunately, no segments of the size that needed replacement were available, so they would have to be newly-cast, although it was thought that timbering could be used in the meantime, if the station were to remain open for passengers.

On the same day as Mount's visit, the LPTB's Chief Engineer submitted a more detailed report on the damage:

There are thirty rings of the disused 10-foot diameter passageway badly damaged alongside the lower escalator chamber and several top segments are fallen in.

The lower escalator chamber and passage are unsafe until properly supported. In the running tunnels below on the NB side the damage is confined to several single cable brackets broken and some breaks in the track concrete haunchings.

On the SB side the joints of the running tunnel have started in a number of places and the top flange of one of the segments is cracked below a chute opening in the floor of the above mentioned 10-foot disused passage.

Some loose concrete in the chute has been removed and some small amount of water is leaking from the soffite of the tunnel.

These running tunnels are considered safe for traffic meantime with a speed restriction which will be imposed.[3]

In the event, full services resumed after twenty-nine days, on 11 November.[4]

Bounds Green Station – 13 October 1940

At 9.15 p.m., a bomb from a lone enemy aircraft demolished two houses directly above the east end of the westbound platform tunnel of Bounds Green Piccadilly line station, killing or mortally wounding seventeen shelterers (see Appendix 1).

At 11 a.m. on 14 October, Lt. Col. Mount of the Ministry of Transport inspected the bomb site and later reported:

Bounds Green station today – the flats on the extreme left were built on the site of the houses demolished by the bomb.

At about 21.17 on 13/10, a heavy bomb (500 kilo?) fell on two houses (Cranbrook) in Bounds Green Road, some 120 to 130 yards north of Bounds Green Station booking hall. The houses (not the Board's property) were completely demolished, killing four people and a huge crater was formed, 60 to 70 feet diameter and depth being about 20 feet. This was immediately above the north end of the southbound platform, where the tunnel is 21 feet 1½ inches diameter, the top of it being 37 feet below the surface; the tunnel iron was 1¼ inches thick.

The station building was not affected and the escalators (51.88 feet rise) remained running; nor was the lighting affected. The top twenty-two segments of the platform tunnel, immediately under the crater, were broken in and clay and debris fell through the hole, some 40 x 20 feet, thus formed in the roof. Some 200 tons of debris filled the tunnel, enveloping [shelterers] on the platform, seventeen of whom were killed and fifty-nine injured; it is estimated that twelve to fifteen are still buried and a temporary tunnel in iron will be commenced tonight at platform level to extricate the bodies.

The adjoining northbound tunnel was evidently shaken and moved, longitudinal cracks being apparent in the tiling and concrete filling. The platform nosing at the north end was also shifted 3 inches towards the track, which gives an idea of the vibratory movement. The platform had already been realigned in cement by the Board's staff and the track appears fit for traffic; but it will be unsafe to put it into operation on account of the instability of the crater debris and until the loose muck is secured it seems unlikely that the northbound line can be opened, say, for ten days.

He also noted:

The attack cannot have been directed towards the Tube and the hit must have been fortuitous; it appears that the enemy was attempting to cut off King's Cross, by hitting the south end of the LNER main line tunnel between Wood Green Station and New Southgate, the south end of the tunnel being only a few hundred yards to the west of Bounds Green Station. The main line here has ordinary signals and not colour-lights, but there was brilliant moonlight. This appears to be the only explanation as there is no aerodrome nearby.

Added by hand to Mount's report was: 'This is the sixth bomb damage to Tube tunnelling.' The damage was so extensive that it was decided that the only way to tackle it would be to expand the crater into a timber-lined trench covering the whole width of the damaged platform tunnel, which could then be rebuilt, before being covered over again. Mount estimated that this would require, 'some 4,000 running feet of 12 x 12-foot and 14 x 14-foot timbers, at least 34 feet long.'[5]

Repairs were started on 25 October and completed on 12 December. Traffic was running again four days later and the site cleared the following day.[6]

Balham station – 14 October 1940

At 8.02 p.m., a 1,400 kg 'Esau' semi-armour piercing bomb struck the road surface in front of 184 Balham High Road, just north of Balham Northern line station. Penetrating deeply before detonating, the bomb only exploded when it hit the cast iron segments of a cross passageway, causing a massive crater on the surface and collapsing the northern end of the north-bound platform tunnel. An avalanche of earth, debris and water from broken mains and sewers flooded into the station, which was packed with people sheltering from the air raid, causing multiple fatalities (see Appendix 1). The running tunnels between Clapham South and Tooting Bec stations were also flooded. Southbound trains were reversed at Clapham Common, with current off south of the latter station to Morden.[7, 8, 9, 10]

At 12 p.m. on 15 October, Lt. Col. Mount visited the bomb site and later reported:

At 20.02 hours (precisely) on 14/10, a heavy bomb (presumably 500 kilo?) fell on the north-bound tramway track in Balham high Road, some 200 yards north of the Southern Railway main (Brighton) line four-track bridge over this road, 1½ miles [2.4 km] south east of Clapham Junction and the same distance north west of Streatham.

This site was immediately over the north end of the north-bound tube platform where the tunnel lining is 22 feet 1½ inches diameter and about 27 feet below the surface of the road. The top of the tunnel was broken in to an extent which is at present unknown; the south side of the fracture being located some 18 feet north of the platform clock. The road carried three 30-inch water mains and one of 10 inches; also a 4 feet x 2 feet 8 inches sewer and two gas mains 6 inches and 8 inches. All the mains were broken as also many cable and of course the tram lines. A large quantity of shingle, silt and water and some clay ran through the cavity into the tunnel with the result that the final crater extended completely across the road from shop to shop, its diameter being some 60 to 70 feet. A north-bound No. 88 bus had pitched headlong into it at a steep angle, the conductor's platform coming to rest just above the level of the roadway. It will be a big operation in itself to get the bus out.

Entering the station via the escalators, we walked through the sliding watertight door on to the shingle and silt covered platform and up to the bottom of the crater through which there was daylight; the depth of the shingle and silt over the platform was 4 or 5 feet tapering off to nothing at the south end of the platform. The Stationmaster's office was located at the north end of this platform on the north side of the crater, but we did not inspect that side and at present I have not heard whether anyone has done so. The shingle had flowed out through the one sliding and one hinged watertight doors on this platform into the escalator chamber. There is another sliding watertight door from this chamber giving access to the south-bound platform through which the Fire Brigade were pumping out this tunnel. Water was still draining from one of the mains into the crater like a small waterfall.

With regard to the unprecedented loss of life, Mount appeared to be hoping for the best, or rather the least-worst:

The massive crater over the collapsed platform tunnel at Balham station, and the same view today. This is the same incident shown on page 102.

With the police, we interviewed Mrs F. Chalmers of 20 Southey Road, Kennington, who was accustomed, with her friends, to shelter at the south end of the north-bound platform. We gathered that, after hearing the bomb, she felt no blast (and she had had experience of bomb blast), but the lights went out. She was certain that the watertight doors were closed and that members of the public immediately opened them, the rush of water and shingle being heard; in the darkness they were able to get away from the platform and Mrs Chalmer's general impression seemed to be that few were left behind. The numbers taking shelter were apparently normal. Mrs Chalmers referred to the Stationmaster and his relations who were usually collected near his office and she thought they must have been buried.

No. 5 Group Co-Ordinating Officer, Civil Defence, informed us that his reports up to date varied from twelve to twenty-two dead and he thought forty to fifty was an outside guess for those who had been caught under the debris. It must depend largely upon how closely people were lying.

Some digging had already been undertaken in the search for bodies, but I think the suggested figure of 200 is clearly an exaggeration and, having regard to the comparative slowness with which the shingle, silt and water must have come in, I shall be surprised if the numbers killed are not considerably less than the above-mentioned guess.

By 6 December, Mount reported that repairs were progressing well and that it might be possible to have the tunnels open to traffic again before Christmas, but bodies were still being recovered. He visited the site again on 13 December and noted that the water mains and sewer destroyed by the explosion had been rebuilt, but the contamination of the site and number of bodies still in situ had made for difficult working conditions:

The men are now working under better conditions and gas masks are no longer being used; disinfectants are plentiful and I understand there has been no undue sickness. Having regard to the conditions, the men receive an additional allowance. By means of tarpaulins over the top of the shaft, operations are being carried on continuously; some sixty men are working by day and thirty by night.

Up to date, some forty bodies have been accounted for, but a considerable number (I gather perhaps twenty or more) still remain to be recovered from the invert under the platform; also from the cross-passage on which the bomb fell.

With regard to the bomb itself, Mount noted:

Wing-Commander Lowe today examined the piece of the bomb in my office and stated that it was of 1,400 kilo type, semi armour piercing, overall length 10 feet, diameter 22.3 inches. The same type of bomb was responsible for the damage at Sloane Square [see below]. Many other smaller fragments have been collected from inside the tunnel and there seems to be no doubt that the bomb fell at an angle, west to east and exploded on hitting the lintel girders of the 11-foot 8½-inch cross-passage at its junction with the North-bound tunnel, some 32 feet below surface.

The more the site was cleared, however, the more apparent it became that the earlier estimate that work could be completed by Christmas was overly optimistic and it was more likely to be the middle of January. Total expenditure was expected to be 'in the order of £25,000 to £30,000, perhaps more' (£3.3 to £4 million today). In the event, traffic through the station resumed on 8 January 1941, with the station itself reopening on the 19th.

Euston Station – 21 October 1940

At 10.16 p.m., a High Explosive bomb hit the road surface at the junction of Eversholt Street and Phoenix Road, fracturing the Northern line tunnels between Mornington Crescent and Euston. Water from broken mains entering the tunnel caused a power surge, tripping high-tension cables at Leicester Square, Belsize Park and Golders Green. A gas main was also fractured and the tunnels filled with debris. Services suspended between Strand (now Charing Cross) and Mornington Crescent.[11][12][13][14]

At 3 p.m. on the 22nd, Lt. Col. Mount visited the bomb site and later reported:

At 10.10 p.m. on 21/10, one or more H.E. bombs (probably 500 kilo) fell and exploded in the centre of the street (wood blocks on concrete) at the junction of Eversholt Street and Phoenix Street (a continuation of Seymour Street) immediately outside the Eastern boundary of Euston Station and 100 yards south of the R.C.H. [Railway Clearing House]. I understand that this was a deliberate dive bombing attack on Euston from just above the balloon barrage.

The crater was about 55 feet diameter and 23 feet deep, going down to the London Clay, the cover above the two 12 feet 7 inches diameter tube running tunnels being about 44 feet. The roofs of both tunnels were broken in to an extent which it is impossible at present to estimate at points about 200 yards north of Euston Tube Station and debris ran into both tunnels. (Iron of 12 feet 7 inches diameter is not standard and therefore will have to be cast specially.)

Water mains of 16 inches, 6 inches and 4 inches were fractured and before they could be closed (1½ hours?) water ran into the tunnels, flooded the suicide pits in the station and flowed southwards through the tunnel into the dip on the north side of Warren Street; but at no place were the tunnels flooded to a serious depth and I understand that the station pumps (automatic) held the water, pending the provision of emergency pumping appliances.

Despite this extensive damage, Mount noted that things could have been even worse:

A train on the south-bound road had just passed the point of damage when the explosion occurred and windows in the rear part of the train were broken. Fortunately there were no casualties and [shelterers] were cleared out of the station as a precautionary measure. Five trains were shut in between Euston and the river and will have to be worked back to Kennington by opening the floodgates. It is proposed, however, to retain one train in each tunnel in order to work a shuttle service between Euston and Strand.

Repairs were initially handled by civilian contractors, but a shortage of workers meant that this work did not begin immediately and when it did, it was quickly handed over to half of the 173rd Tunnelling Company, Royal Engineers, under the command of a Captain Lander, on 5 November. Lander had previously worked as an engineer on the Underground and by 13 November Mount was able to report:

> The Company had made good progress, 7 or 8 rings of a 7-foot pilot tunnel having been erected in the one tunnel. The face had dried out considerably and appeared to be more consolidated than was anticipated. Captain Lander said that a flagstone or two had been met besides a quantity of tunnel iron.
>
> In breaking away a piece of tunnel iron, the previous shift had cut a Post Office telephone cable which was located just outside the pilot iron. Post Office Engineers were making an examination at the same time and were effecting repairs. Below the cable was one of the main secret Post Office telephone cables, which was also fouling the pilot iron. Another cable was apparently cut as a result of the accident.

Traffic resumed on 22 February 1941, after reconstruction of thirty-four rings of iron in one tunnel and forty-one rings in the other. On 28 February the civilian contractors sent Mount a piece of the bomb that had been uncovered during the repair work. Mount invited Wing Commander J. C. M. Lowe of the Ministry of Home Security to examine the find, which he was able to on 5 March, judging it to be from a 500 kilo device, but the large size of the piece suggested that the casing was weak due to poor manufacture and it had fractured before detonation was fully complete.[15, 16, 17]

IN MEMORY OF
THE SIXTEEN BELGIAN REFUGEES AND THE THREE BRITISH CITIZENS
WHO DIED ON THIS PLATFORM DURING THE AIR RAID OF
13 OCTOBER 1940

LONDON UNDERGROUND LIMITED
13 OCTOBER 1994

Memorial plaque on the platform of Bounds Green station.

The devastation at Sloane Square station.

Sloane Square Station – 12 November 1940

A large calibre bomb scored a direct hit on Sloane Square station at 9.50 p.m., causing extensive damage to the ticket hall and platforms. High-tension, signal and lighting cables were also damaged. Two gas mains were severed and set on fire. Initial reports described the rear car of a train standing at the platform as being, 'cut in two,' that forty people had been killed and twenty injured enough to require treatment on-site The following day the casualty figures were revised to twenty-eight killed and forty to fifty injured.[18, 19]

At 10 a.m. on 13 November, Lt. Col. Mount visited the bomb site, along with the LPTB's Engineer-in-Chief, V. A. M. Robertson, and other Board staff and later reported:

At 9.45 pm on 12/11, an H.E. bomb (250 kilo?) hit the booking hall and exploded on contact with the main girder supporting it and nearest to the tunnel. Three or four of the adjacent main girders were also damaged and a portion of the tunnel arch (five rings) was blown away. The whole of the booking hall, a single storey building but of sufficient strength to carry a ten-storey building proposed for future erection, was demolished, the side walls of the station being blown outwards. The escalators on each side were wrecked, as also much of the station roof.

These works have only recently been completed at a cost of about £70,000 (verified later £72,000).

He noted that the bomb exploded some 100 feet from an 8-foot main sewer, which could have potentially released five million cubic feet of water into the tunnel. This had not happened, but the severed gas mains had made rescue work so difficult that it had to be done via the tunnel to South Kensington, rather than directly through the station.

> The debris enveloped an outgoing six-car west-bound train, completely wrecking it and killing passengers therein. A number of other passengers were also killed in the booking hall and possibly on both platforms, making a provisional total of twenty-two. In addition, nine of the Traffic Operating Staff and nine of the Board's Bus Staff were apparently killed in the adjacent mess room, making a total of approximately forty deaths; in addition, fourteen persons are also reported as injured.

It was estimated that it would take some six days to clear the line for traffic and the contractors – Mowlem's – had already started the work, although they had requested additional manpower from the 691st Company, Pioneer Corps.

On 28 November, Mount reported that a 10-ton crane with a 100-foot reach had been brought in to remove the roof girders, escalators and other debris. Although sagging, the cross girders were judged strong enough to support a temporary ticket hall and staircases were to be provided from pavement level. It was anticipated that the station could re-open in a few more days, although some roof covering had yet to be provided. Mount detailed the work done thus far:

> The clearance of the track was effected by 25/11, namely in twelve working days, 7.30 a.m. till 5.30 p.m., 120 working hours, with a force of labour varying from a minimum of sixty to a maximum of 140 – equivalent to some 11,000 man hours.

It was later determined that rather than being a 250 kg device, it had actually been a 1,400 kg semi-armour piercing bomb – the same type that caused so much destruction at Balham a month previously.[20] The final death toll was thirty-seven (see Appendix 1).

Bank station – 11 January 1941

At 7.59 p.m. at Bank station, a HE pierced the road surface and the Central line ticket hall and exploded in the escalator machine room. The blast carried down the escalators and through the open watertight doors to the platforms. People who had been sheltering on the escalators were blown onto the platforms on the one side, where a train was already present and onto the track on the other and some were almost immediately run over by an incoming train before the emergency brakes applied by the driver could fully stop it. The blast also blew upwards and then collapsed the steel girder roof of the ticket hall and subways that supported the road junction, creating an elliptical hole some 200 feet long and 120 feet wide. The initial Civil Defence Region report described the immediate situation:

At the foot of the escalator to the Central London railway there are two steel doors for the prevention of floods giving access to each side of the tube platforms. These doors were open and the main casualties were those sheltering at the foot of the escalator, who were blown through the doors against the wall of the tube opposite. Had these doors been shut, the technical officer of the Transport Board advises that the blast might have blown in the sides of the tube tunnels.[21]

The bomb essentially created two separate incident sites: the crater on the surface and – effectively cut off from it – the damage and casualties at platform level. The first rescue workers were on the scene by 8.03, but could only deal with the situation on the surface. Down below, shelterers were cleared from the platforms via the connecting passageways to the Northern line platforms, while the only doctor on duty – Hungarian refugee Z. A. Leitner – did his best to triage and treat the casualties with rapidly dwindling medical supplies for an hour and a half before other doctors could relieve him from the surface. Eventually four rescue parties were at the site, along with two stretcher parties, 15 Company of the Pioneer Corps and officers and twenty-eight men of 691 General Construction Company of the Royal Engineers.

Despite the scale of devastation, the running tunnels themselves were not affected, so through services resumed the following day. The shattered ticket hall was another matter and the road junction of such importance that the Royal Engineers spanned the chasm with a temporary girder bridge. This allowed the traffic to flow again, while the road surface was gradually reinstated.

The huge crater caused by the collapsing ticket hall at Bank station.

Another view of the crater at Bank and, below, the same location today.

The subsequent inquiry noted a number of issues that had hampered rescue and medical work, such as the need for temporary lighting separate from the LPTB's power supply, more medical supplies in shelters and a better enforcement on the prohibition on sheltering in ticket halls and on escalators. After giving his evidence to the inquiry, Dr Leitner stated:

I should like to make a remark. You English people cannot appreciate the discipline of your own people. I want to tell you I have not found one hysterical patient. I think this is very important, that you should not take such things as given, because it does not happen in other countries. If Hitler could have been there for five minutes with me he would have finished this war. He would have realised that he has got to take every Englishman and twist him by the neck – otherwise he cannot win this war.

The final death toll was at least fifty-six (see Appendix 1).

Bethnal Green – 3 March 1943

While used by as many as 7,000 people during the intensive bombing of 1940–41, by 1943, demand at the Bethnal Green shelter had declined to around just 200–300 each night, rising only in the days following reported heavy Allied raids on Berlin, when retaliatory bombing on London was anticipated. On 2 March it was reported that there had been a heavy raid on Berlin the day before, with the result that 850 people used the shelter that night. At 8.17 p.m. on the 3rd, the alert sounded and people began to enter the shelter – initially in a calm and orderly fashion – to join the 500–600 already inside.

At 8.27, a salvo of a new type of anti-aircraft rocket was launched one-third of a mile away. Some people in the street threw themselves to the ground in reaction to the unfamiliar sound, while the crowd entering the shelter surged forwards. Whether as a result of this – or coincidental with it – a woman with a child tripped at the bottom of the nineteen-step stairway leading down from the pavement entrance to the booking hall. In the resultant crush, 172 people suffocated and of those admitted to hospital, one subsequently died and sixty-two were retained overnight, only thirty of them being discharged within the following week.

Although subsequent Nazi propaganda radio broadcasts cited it as an example of 'panic' among Londoners in reaction to German bombing, the hastily-convened Government inquiry into the tragedy came to the conclusion that the single entrance to the shelter – being at an angle to the adjacent pavement – was a natural bottleneck that allowed more people to enter than the stairway could accommodate in such a surge, while the lack of adequate lighting and crush-barriers to restrict the flow had contributed to the tragedy. It was recognised that while there was not sufficient police or shelter warden provision, this was not unique to Bethnal Green, but was rather the result of the overall shortage of manpower in light of the numbers called up for the armed services.

It is something of a fallacy that news of the incident was 'censored' or 'suppressed.' While it is true that publication of the Inquiry's report was delayed until after the war, its proceedings were public and reported at the time, as was the disaster itself. The *Daily*

Worker in particular, printed frequent reports and even *The Illustrated London News* featured photographs of the Inquiry members visiting the shelter.

Chapter six References:

1. AN 2/1105.
2. MT 6/2759.
3. MT 6/2759.
4. HO 186/2419.
5. MT 6/2766.
6. MT 6/2759.
7. AN 2/1105.
8. HO 201/3.
9. MT 6/2759.
10. AN 2/1105.
11. AN 2/1105.
12. HO 201/3.
13. AN 2/1105.
14. HO 192/8.
15. HO 196/11.
16. MT 6/2759.
17. MT 6/2766.
18. AN 2/1106.
19. HO 201/4.
20. MT 6/2759.
21. HO186/639.

The north portal of Highgate North Tunnel, damaged at 10.33 p.m. on 19 April 1941. The original brickwork was hastily repaired with Tube tunnel segments

CHAPTER 7

AFTERMATH

Even while the capital was still under sporadic air attack, the County of London published the *County of London Plan 1943* by J. H. Forshaw and Professor Patrick Abercrombie. It represented an ambitious blueprint for the planned and orderly London that would – or at least they thought *should* – rise from the Blitzed rubble of the War. In this they rejected what had been the standard model for the expansion of the Underground in the past:

> We do not favour the policy of extension of the tube system in order to open up new ground for further loads on routes which are already taxed beyond their capacity. An attempt should be made to diminish the need for so much pendulum travel. [One step] is in the direction of improving the existing tube and suburban rail system. The tube system requires greater ease of movement at the centre, allowing trains to run more frequently in special hours and to return by means of inner circles or loops. The possibilities of a duplication of tubes on certain lines or some other means of providing an express service need exploring.[135]

They suggested the elimination of rail bridges over the Thames, with Charing Cross, Canon Street, and Blackfriars mainline stations replaced with deep tube stations below the same sites, serving the new tube 'circles or loops.'

In 1945 the government published the *Greater London Plan 1944*, Abercrombie's single-handed follow-up. He expanded his theory of avoiding the remorseless expansion of London proper, instead advocating the creation of new satellite towns further out, with good transport links to the Metropolis by road and rail. One candidate for such development was the small market town of Chipping Ongar, centred on the railway station that was due to become the new eastern terminus of the Central line. Abercrombie even recommended that the line be extended on to Chelmsford, and estimated that the new town could accommodate a population of 60,000. An earlier consideration – rejected due to proximity to North Weald Aerodrome and a radio station – had placed the new town between North Weald and Blake Hall stations, but while no direct connection was planned, even the final Ongar version would have its western edge just over a third of a mile from Blake Hall.

The hydrophones are removed from the Thames.

Land for the Underground extensions which had been shelved by the coming of the war was used to grow vegetables for the LPTB staff canteen.

The decaying remains of Highgate High-Level station.

Ultimately while some of Abercrombie's new towns were built, Ongar was not one of them, so the expected demand for the Epping–Ongar section of the Central line never materialised. It operated for years as a shuttle service and in 1981 Blake Hall fell victim to the staggeringly low usage of, allegedly, six passengers a day, before the whole section was shut down in 1994. It now operates as a heritage railway, with the line severed short of Epping, which remains in Underground use.

Apart from the completion of the Central line extensions (the western one stopped one station short of the intended terminus at Denham), there was no real peace dividend for the Underground. The Northern Heights part of the New Works Programme was quietly shelved, and the work done before suspension written off. The LNER and then British Rail continued steam passenger services on the Finsbury Park–Alexandra Palace branch until 1954, and freight until 1964. Most of the track-bed now forms the Parkland Walk, with only the ghostly surviving platforms at Crouch End and the gated southern end of the Highgate South Tunnel betraying its original use. At this point, walkers have to climb up to Archway Road, from where the northern end of Highgate North Tunnel – the patched bomb damage it suffered on 19 April 1944 still discernible – can be seen through the trees. A detour to the entrance of Highgate low-level station in Priory Gardens allows for a glimpse of the crumbling high-level platforms built for – but unused by – Underground trains.

The single-track line from Finchley Central to Edgware was similarly used for freight services until 1964, but Northern line trains never got past Mill Hill East, although as late as 1969 street atlases still showed Mill Hill (The Hale) as an Underground station, albeit a closed one. Mill Hill East remains a historical oddity, but beyond Edgware the viaduct arches that would have supported Brockley Hill station have been reduced to mere stumps alongside the Watford By-Pass, while the building of the M1 obliterated the tunnels that would have taken the line through the hill to Elstree South and on to Bushey Heath. Ambitious though the stations beyond Edgware would have been, in retrospect it seems possible that with Green Belt legislation preventing residential development around the stations, they too might have fallen to the same fate as North Weald, Blake Hall, and Ongar.

Today, three-quarters of a century from the start of the Second World War, the London Underground bears her scars quietly and unobtrusively. A memorial here, a long-seized flood-gate there and tell-tale scraps of discontinuity in tiling, or brickwork, or tunnel. Traces of wartime damage to – and service by – the oldest underground railway system in the world, in the greatest city in the world.

As this book is being written, giant tunnel boring machines – the descendants of Barlow and Greathead's tunnelling shields, with Brunel's as a distant relative – are carving their way under London constructing Crossrail, the capital's next generation tube railway …

Appendix 1

CIVILIAN FATALITIES LINKED TO THE LONDON UNDERGROUND DUE TO WAR OPERATIONS

The purpose of these pages is to reconcile the various previously published figures for casualties and fatalities associated with the London Underground network during the Second World War with the register of Civilian War Dead maintained by the Commonwealth War Graves Commission (CWGC), and where possible to identify those killed by name.

It is important to note that throughout the War a series of government schemes existed to pay pensions and other compensation to the relatives or dependents of those civilians killed or injured 'due to war operations.' In the context of the subject of this book, this would include anyone killed directly or indirectly by enemy weapons (i.e. bombs or gunfire), but also by accidental death due to Allied weapons. Someone killed by the blast of an enemy bomb would be covered, as would someone killed by a falling British anti-aircraft shell, but someone merely run over by a vehicle (official or otherwise) in the blackout would not. Civilian deaths due to war operations were thus very extensively and accurately documented at local borough or district level and these records formed the basic of the Commission's register.

Balham – 14 October 1940

The reported number of fatalities for this incident usually varies between sixty-four and sixty-eight, although until recently the CWGC recorded sixty-five. For many years a plaque in the station ticket hall gave the total as sixty-four, which led to speculation that four LPTB staff had been excluded from the supposed total of sixty-eight. However, as the CWGC records included stationmaster John Rundle, it seems unlikely that they did not also include the other three putative members of staff.

In May 2010 a previously unrecorded casualty was added to the CWGC register, making the total up to sixty-six. In October the same year, the plaque in the ticket hall was replaced with one commemorating, 'the civilians and London Transport staff who were

The currently incomplete Stairway to Heaven memorial, with the entrance to Bethnal Green station on the other side of the railings

killed at this station during the Blitz on the night of 14 October 1940,' without numbering them.

14 October 1940 – 'Died at Balham tube station' (Metropolitan Borough of Wandsworth):

Ballam, Frances Sarah (age 55)
Ballam, Margaret Emily (age 26)
Ballam, Percy Frederick (age 55)
Baxendine, Alice (age 26)
Baxendine, James Charles (age 26)
Bell, Clarence Montague (age 42)
Benbrook, Gladys Bessie (age 42)
Boland, Ernest Frederick (age 27)
Brown, Ada Mary (age 41)
Brown, Constance (age 14)
Brown, Harry (age 21)
Brown, Ivy Edith (age 26)
Brown, James William (age 41)
Brown, Joyce (age 12)
Brown, Mary Ann (age 65)
Budd, Caroline Sarah Hilda (age 58)
Budd, Olive Hilda (age 13)
Carey, George Walter (age 57)
Comben, Alfred Joseph (age 48)
Comben, Emma Emily (age 45)
Cottingham, Elizabeth (age 55)
Cottingham, Joseph William (age 53)
Courtney, Bridget (age 49)
Courtney, Mary (age 26)
Dibble, Roy John (age 7)
Dobbs, Frederick James (age 41)
Dudley, Frederick Arthur (age 34)
Flack, Emily Ann (age 47)
Flack, Winifred Mary (age 20)
Graham, Samuel (age 26)
Greenhead, Albert (age 32)
Hall, Edward John (age 40)
Harrison, Arthur Edwin (age 43)
Harrison, Ethel Olive (age 46)
Harrison, Joan (age 20)
Harrison, Kathleen Olive (age 16)
Harrison, Patricia (age 13)
Heron, Elsie Irene (age 47)

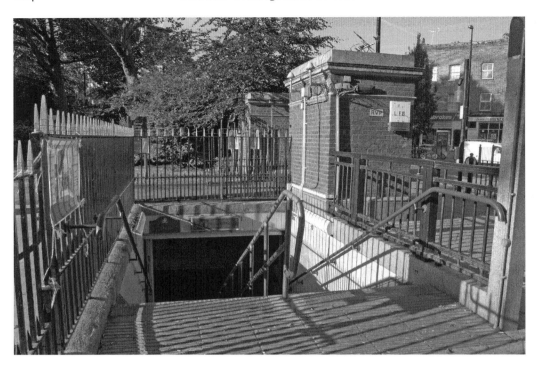

The entrance at Bethnal Green where so many died. Below, the memorial plaque above the entrance to the station.

Heron, Frederick William John (age 24)
Heron, John (age 47)
Hyde, George Francis (age 60)
Hyde, Irene Louisa (age 37)
Lyle, Grace (age 14)
Lyle, Margaret Grace (age 59)
Mansfield, Iris Audrey (age 19)
Mansfield, Nellie Grace (age 5)
Miller, Caroline Elizabeth (age 52)
Neal, Lawrence Archibald (age 45)
Neal, Marie Clare (age 16)
Neal, Sarah (age 45)
Neal, Sidney (age 19)
Palmer, Emily Louisa (age 37)
Palmer, Thomas Samuel (age 63)
Parrish, James William (age 54)
Ravening, Elsie Mary (age 35)
Ravening, Michael John Anthony (age 4)
Rhind, Daisy Bertha (age 40)
Rundle, John (age 64) [Station Master][1]
Sexton, Alfred Robert James (age 46)
Sexton, Arthur George (age 4)
Sexton, Maud Alice Rose (age 34)
Shopland, Leonard George (age 38)
Trudgill, Mornington Sydney (age 35)
Welsh, Francis Patrick (age 19)
Willer, Mary Helen (age 50)
Wilson, Edith (age 51)

Bank – 11 January 1941

In the immediate aftermath of this incident, the number of casualties was reported as:

Dead – twenty-five bodies recovered
Ten more believed still to be under debris
Taken to hospital – forty
Slightly injured – sixty[2]

Most accounts state fifty-six killed and sixty-nine wounded, giving a total of 125, rather than the 135 estimated above. The CWGC records fifty-six civilian fatalities related to 'Bank tube station.' Of these, forty-six were immediate deaths in situ, while nine died in hospital, either the same night or over the next two days.

11 January 1941 – 'Died at Bank tube station' (City of London):

Barritt, Kate (age 49) [WVS Worker]
Beagles, Arthur William (age 25) [Constable, City of London Police]
Beckett, Elizabeth Florence (age 48)
Beckett, Ernest William (age 58)
Blackeby, Augustus George (age 59)
Blake, Peter Cecil (age 17)
Block, David (age 62)
Bond, Royston Sidney (age 34)
Brown, Herbert Arthur (age 14)
Brown, William Charles (age 45)
Burlison, James Richard (age 59)
Cavanagh, Edward John (age 54)
Cumine, George James Gordon Gerald, D.S.O. (age 59)
Free, Robert William (age 48)
Gates, Arnold George (age 35)
Goodwin, Charles Alfred (age 16)
Gregory, Alice (age 41)
Gregory, Corrine (age 14)
Griffiths, William (age 70)
Hall, Benjamin (age 39)
Harrison, James David (age 65)
Heard, John George (age 33) [Constable, Police War Reserve]
James, Ambrose Gerard (age 34)
Kappes, Ellen Elizabeth (age 15)
Krise, George Ernest (age 27)
Lawrence, Harold Alexander (age 39)
Leyserman, Alida (age 28)
Messer, Frederick (age 39)
Milano, Filippo (age 52) [Italian national]
Roast, Harry (age 16)
Sawyer, Stanley Philip (age 18)
Silverstein, Morris (age 57) [otherwise Silverstone]
Smart, Albert Victor (age 45)
Smart, Annie Grace (age 43)
Smith, Edward Julien (age 47)
Smith, Louisa (age 46)
Sole, Charles Arthur (age 17)
Soley, Bernard Henry (age 18)
Such, Emanuel (age 18)
Travitz, Jack (age 44) [otherwise Gravitz]
Tulloch, David (age 61)
Waldron, Charles Henry (age 30)

Wells, Alice Maud (age 62)
Wilcox, Frank Edward (age 17) [Home Guard]
Winsky, Rene (age 14)
Ziff, Hannah Fanny (age 60) [Russian national]

11 January 1941 – 'Injured at Bank tube station; died same day at St Bartholomew's Hospital' (City of London):

Fosh, Ronald Walter (age 14)
Gates, Sheila (age 5)
Josephovitch, Abraham (age 32)
Katz, Celia (age 24) ['Near St Bartholomew's Hospital']

11 January 1941 – 'Injured at Bank station; died same day at London Hospital' (Metropolitan Borough of Stepney):

Bochner, Max (age 49) [Polish citizen]

11 January 1941 – 'Injured at Bank tube station; died same day at London Hospital' (Metropolitan Borough of Stepney):

Pruijm, David (age 60) [Netherlands subject]

12 January 1941 – 'Injured 11 January 1941, at Bank tube station; died at St Bartholomew's Hospital' (City of London):

Hemming, Winifred Lilian (age 24)
Smith, Alice Augusta (age 68)

12 January 1941 – 'Injured 11 January 1941, at Bank tube station; died at London Hospital' (Metropolitan Borough of Stepney):

Payne, Ellen (age 35)

13 January 1941 – 'Injured 11 January 1941, at Bank tube station; died at London Hospital' (Metropolitan Borough of Stepney):

Gates, Albert William (age 28)

Of the above, one was a Women's Voluntary Service (WVS) worker, one a member of the Home Guard and two were police constables. References to the number of fatalities being, 'fifty-three shelterers,' may be attributed to three of these four being 'on duty' at the time.

The CWGC records numerous other casualties as a result of the same air raid at locations including Liverpool Street Station (mainline), Bishopsgate, Bishopgate Street, and New

Street. Two fatalities are recorded at the Mansion House, adjacent to Bank Station. All bar one of those who subsequently died in hospital have the location where they were injured recorded. The single exception, however, shares a surname and a Bethnal Green home address with a known Bank fatality, and so may be a 'missing' fifty-seventh victim:

19 January 1941 – 'died at St Bartholomew's Hospital' (City of London):

Leyserman, Martha (age 29)

Bounds Green – 13 October 1940

The number of fatalities usually stated for this incident is nineteen, frequently described by nationality in accordance with the description given in London Transport's official history of the War:

> In fact, nineteen people were killed, all except three of whom were Belgians. A local colony of refugees from Belgium had ensconced themselves at the far end of the west platform on the first night of the blitz. They kept themselves to themselves, and it was only because they had been blitzed out of two homes in forty-eight hours that the foreman ticket-collector had permitted three British subjects to shelter in the Belgians' section of the platform.[3]

The CWGC records, however, cast doubt on certain aspects of the above account:

13 October 1940 – 'Died at tube station, Bounds Green Road' (Municipal Borough of Wood Green):

Boulle, Francine (age 5) [Belgian subject]
Jemmett, Albert George (age 67)
Jemmett, Charlotte Sarah (age 58)
Jemmett, Florence May (age 23)
Kingate, Henry Mark (age 59)
Mandall, Henry Mark (age 8)
Mandall, Pauline Louise (age 18 months)
Mandall, Rachael Louise (age 11)
Mears, Winifred Jessie (age 35) [WVS worker]
Necchi, Giulio (age 9)
Necchi, Mafalda (age 15)
Necchi, Mark John (age 41)
Necchi, Rose (age 40)
Watts, Ellen Mary (age 64)

14 October 1940 – 'Died at tube station, Bounds Green Road' (Municipal Borough of Wood Green):

Neuckermans, Robert Joseph Auguste (age 26) [Belgian subject]
Van Haelter, David (age 28) [Belgian subject]

14 October 1940 – 'Injured 13 October 1940, at tube station, Bounds Green Road; died at Friern Emergency Hospital' (Urban District of Friern Barnet):

Mandall, William Alfred (age 33)

As can be seen, only three of the above are identified as being Belgian, but of the remaining thirteen recorded as having died at the station, nine do not have names that would suggest them being anything other than British. This leaves the four members of the Necchi family, but the surname is Italian and the forenames of the two adults suggest that they were not recent immigrants to the UK.

It seems likely that this is simply a case of the number of casualties being confused at some point, and it was in fact thirteen British citizens and three Belgians who were killed on the night itself – 'sixteen plus three ...' being mistaken for 'sixteen, of whom three...'

As to the story about the 'English family' recently arrive in the area, the following are the home addresses for the victims, together with their approximate distances from the station:

Boulle – 47 Palace Gates Road [1km]
Jemmett (3) – 93 Bowes Road, Southgate [1 km]
Kingate – 38 Park Avenue [1km]
Mandall (3) - 38 Park Avenue [1km]
Mears – 145 Petherton Road, Highbury [6.4 km]
Necchi (4) – 50 Oakley Road, Islington [7.8 km]
Neuckermans – 5 Braemar Avenue [0.9 km]
Van Haelter – 90 Arcadian Gardens [3.7 km]
Watts – 86 Evesham Road, Southgate [0.8 km]

Since Winifred Mears was in attendance as a WVS (Women's Voluntary Service) worker, she is an exception, but it would seem that the Necchi family were those often stated as recently-arrived in the area, having been bombed out of their previous home. References to the family only being three in number are probably an attempted reconciliation with the erroneous belief that only three of the fatalities were British.

In addition, the following four people were killed in the houses demolished by the bomb, which then caused the platform tunnel to collapse:

13 October 1940 – 'Died at Cedars, Bounds Green Road' (Municipal Borough of Wood Green):

Bowdich, Barbara Antoinette (age 11)

Page, Maud Jean (age 35)
Page, Moya (age 16 months)

13 October 40 – 'Died at Cranbrook, Bounds Green Road' (Municipal Borough of Wood Green):

Norris, Charles Victor (age 63)

Camden Town – 14 October 1940

Most sources state a single fatality in this bombing, but the CWGC has five:

14 October 1940 - 'Died at Camden Town tube station' (Metropolitan Borough of St Pancras):

Crook, Henry Edward (age 56)
Hills, Herbert Alfred (age 58)
Makri, Charalambos George (age 28)
Tolly, Patrick (age 65)

14 October 1940 - 'Injured at Camden Town tube station; died same day at National Temperance Hospital' (Metropolitan Borough of St Pancras):

Russell, Alfred James (age 16)

Chalk Farm – 17 April 1941

One known fatality, possibly on duty on station roof:

17 April 1941 – 'Died at Chalk Farm tube station' (Metropolitan Borough of St Pancras):

Catlin, Christopher William (age 29) [Air Raid Warden/Firewatcher]

Chalk Farm – 11 May 1941
Two known fatalities, who again may have been on duty on the station roof:

11 May 1941 – 'Died at Chalk Farm Station' (Metropolitan Borough of St Pancras):

Twohey, John William (age 42) [Railway A.R.P.]
Walton, Howard James (age 44) [Air Raid Warden]

Charing Cross – 8 October 1940

During this incident, a number of High Explosive bombs hit Charing Cross mainline station, passing through the roof of the adjacent Underground station of the same name (the current Embankment). Contemporary documentation notes that one person was killed, and the CWGC records the following:

8 October 1940 – 'Died at Charing Cross Underground station' – (City of Westminster):

Uffindell, Wilfred Samuel (age 30)

In addition, nine people were killed in the mainline station, with a tenth dying in hospital later:

8 October 1940 – 'Died at Charing Cross Southern Railway station' – (City of Westminster):

Baird, Joseph (age 42)
Dowsett, Charles Henry (age 74)
Goldsmith, Walter (age 55)
Quaife, Edwin (age 50)
Tarryer, William Frederick (age 42)
Tully, Frank Edwin (age 42)

8 October 1940 – 'Died at Charing Cross Station' – (City of Westminster):

Bailey, Iris Nina Margaret (age 23)
Foster, Robert Samuel (age 38)
Wheble, Harry (age 50)

17 October 1940 – 'Injured at Charing Cross Station; died at Charing Cross Hospital.' – (City of Westminster):

Collings, William Harry (age 24)

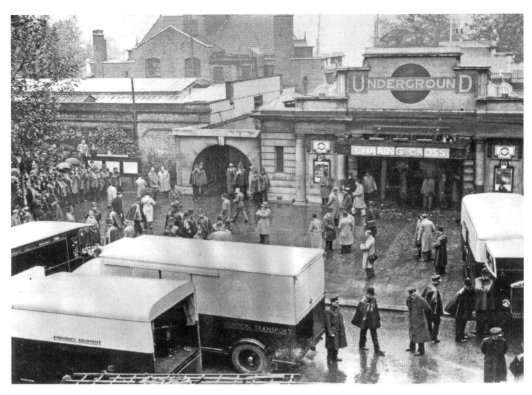

ARP exercise outside the Villiers Street entrance to Charing Cross (now Embankment) station in 1938.

Colindale station as it is today.

Charing Cross – 29 December 1940

29 December 1940 – 'Died at Victoria Embankment, Charing Cross Underground.' – (City of Westminster):

Quinn, Thomas (age 63)

Colindale 25 – September 1940

The station was bombed twice in one night, first at 8.45 p.m., and then again at 10.45. The CWGC records eight fatalities at the scene:

25 September 1940 – 'Died at Colindale station' – (Municipal Borough of Hendon):

Clapp, William James (age 54)
Hunt, William Henry Francis (age 31)
Jenner, Arthur Stanley (age 36)
Moore, Margaret (age 20)
Rood, Elsie May (age 19)
Rosser, David Robert (age 24) [Air Raid Warden]
Shrubb, Walter Thomas (age 44) [Air Raid Warden]
Valler, John Victor (age 29)

East Ham 7 – September 1940

7 September 1940 – 'Died at East Ham Station.' (County Borough of East Ham):

Turner, George (age 5)

Euston Square – 19 September 1940

19/09/1940 – 'Died near Euston Square station' (Metropolitan Borough of St Pancras):

Donoghue, Hugh (age 30)

19/09/40 – 'Injured at Euston Square; died at Middlesex Hospital.' (Metropolitan Borough of St Marylebone):

Shears, Albert (age 32)

Farringdon Street – 16 October 1940

16/10/1940 – 'Died at Farringdon Street station' (Metropolitan Borough of Finsbury):

Cooper, William George (age 43)

Green Park – 11 January 1941

If casualties are noted at all for this bombing, they are usually stated as two LT staff injured, but CWGC records show a higher number:

11 January 1941 – 'Died at Green Park station, Piccadilly' (City of Westminster):

Doig, Dulcie Ida Audrey (age 22) [SRN, Hospital Sister, Acton Hospital]
Langfield, Frederick Curtin (age 42)
Rogan, James (age 34) [Driver, London Auxiliary Ambulance Service]*
Tidman, Estelle Ryall (age 26) [Driver, London Auxiliary Ambulance Service]*
Tolan, Patrick (age 49)
Weight, Marion Jubilee (age 53)

12 January 1941 – 'Injured at Green Park tube station; died same day at West Middlesex County Hospital, Isleworth' (Municipal Borough of Heston and Isleworth):

Levine, Morris (age 57)
* Ambulance drivers 'Paddy' Rogan and 'Blondie' Tidman were eulogised in the *Daily Express* of 13 January 1941. Tidman had been a companion-driver before for the War and had volunteered for the LAAS the previous October. One of her colleagues said: 'Nothing frightened her, nothing made her wince. She was one of those girls who faced anything.' Tidman was found at the wheel of the ambulance outside the station, while Rogan was in the road between her and where the bomb exploded, having evidently been trying to shield her from it.

With thanks to Alex Scott for assistance in expanding details of this incident.

King's Cross – 9 March 1941

One known fatality of a London Underground worker:

9 March 19/41 – 'Died at King's Cross Metro Station' (Metropolitan Borough of St Pancras):

Hill, Stanley Vivian (age 40)
With thanks to David Glennerster for notification of this incident.

Lambeth North – 16 January 1941

Casualties for this bombing are usually stated as twenty injured, while the CWGC records that one subsequently died:

31 January 1941 – 'Injured 15 January 1941, at Lambeth North tube station; died at St. Thomas's Hospital' (Metropolitan Borough of Lambeth):

Garland, Robert Isaac (age 68)

New Cross – 8 September 1940

8 September 1940 – 'Injured 7 September 1940, at New Cross station; died at St Giles Hospital' (Metropolitan Borough of Camberwell):

Shenton, Richard James (age 43) [Engine driver]

Paddington [Praed Street] – 13 October 1940

This bombing resulted in significant loss of life, but was not recorded in previous accounts of high fatality incidents (Graves, etc.):

13 October 1940 – 'Died at Praed Street station' (Metropolitan Borough of Paddington):

Charlemont, Evelyn Fanny Charlotte (age 55)
Moore, George Thomas (age 24)
Murphy, Matthew (age 19)
Murphy, Patrick Joseph (age 16)
Quish, William (age 30)

13 October 1940 – 'Injured at Praed Street station; died same day at St Mary's Hospital' (Metropolitan Borough of Paddington):

Grubb, Emily Matilda (age 33)

14 October 1940 – 'Injured 13 October 1940, at Praed Street station; died at St. Mary's Hospital' (Metropolitan Borough of Paddington):

Coles, Claude (age 30)
Smith, John William (age 29)

24/09/42 – 'Injured 13 October 1940, at Praed Street station; died at 57 Chiltern Street' (Metropolitan Borough of St Marylebone):

    Churchill, Margery Kate (age 33)

In addition to the above eight fatalities, there is a ninth who may have either been injured on the thoroughfare itself, or the 'station' detail was omitted in error, although it is more likely to be the former:

17 October 1940 – 'Injured 13 October 1940, at Praed Street; died at St Mary's Hospital' (Metropolitan Borough of Paddington):

    Brown, Leonard Charles Stewart (age 31)

Sloane Square – 12 Novemeber 1940

A figure of seventy-nine casualties is often applied to this incident, but while some sources give it as the number of injured, with others it is fatalities. The CWGC records thirty-five immediate deaths and two from injuries subsequently:

12 November 1940 – 'Died at Sloane Square station' (Metropolitan Borough of Chelsea):

    Adams, Frederick Victor (age 30)
    Birch, Leonard Albert (age 46)
    Boreham, Florence Audrey (age 32)
    Box, Fred (age 58)
    Bullock, William Charles (age 34)
    Chamberlain, William Henry (age 35)
    Cook, James John (age 37)
    Cooper, George James (age 40)
    Dance, Ambrose John George (age 34)
    Daniels, George Henry Albert (age 33)
    Dingnan, James Patrick (age 32)
    Duce, Edith Rosa (age 53)
    Fox, Ernest (age 40) [Home Guard]
    George, William Hedley (age 35)
    Griffin, Charles (age 39)
    Harding, Albert Henry Russell (age 5?)
    Hawes, Benjamin (age 46)
    Head, Robert George (age 29)
    Henderson, Ada Sophie (age 29)

Hinchcliffe, Charles Thomas (age 29)
Houston, Henry Gordon (age 30)
Jenning, Edward John (age 56)
Knight, Frederick Thomas (age 48)
Lock, Vincent Alfred (age 43)
Loveday, James George Heber (age 50)
Patterson, Albert Edward (age 39) [Home Guard]
Peachey, Ernest Walter (age 48)
Pitt, Elizabeth Ann (age 26)
Reynolds, Alfred (age 46)
Rogers, Silvester George (age 61)
Saunders, Walter William (age 32)
Thompson, Norman Henry (age 31)
Tilbery, Clifford Charles (age 27) [Special Constable]
Walkling, George (age 35)
Waller, Henry (age 33)

13 November 1940 – 'Injured 12 November 1940, at Sloane Square station; died at St Luke's Hospital' (Metropolitan Borough of Chelsea):

Richardson, Arthur (age 36)

28 November 1940 – 'Died at Botleys Park War Hospital' (Urban District of Chertsey):

Lanham, Alfred Edward Ernest (age 25)

St Mary's – 19 April 1941

The station closed to traffic on 30 April 1938, but was being used as a public air raid shelter when bombed in 1941:

19 April 1941 – 'Died at St Mary's railway station, Whitechapel Road' (Metropolitan Borough of Stepney):

Black, Sidney Jack (age 17)
Bull, Percy (age 48) [Firewatcher]
Glick, Harry (age 45) [Russian national]
Levy, Alexander Harris (age 31) [Constable, Police War Reserve]
Silverman, Louis (age 53)
Tree, George Frederick (age 30) [Constable, Police War Reserve]

Stanmore – 13 October 1940

One fatality of a resident in a flat above the station building:

13 October 1940 – 'Injured at Metropolitan station; died same day at Royal National Orthopaedic Hospital, Stanmore' (Harrow Urban District):

   Sargent, Eric Charles (age 32)

Trafalgar Square – 12 October 1940

The usual figure of seven fatalities for this incident is confirmed by the CWGC, although all bar one of them refer to merely 'Trafalgar Square station,' rather than the 'Tube station' of the seventh:

12 October 1940 – 'Died at Trafalgar Square station' (City of Westminster):

   Berstad, Sigvart (age 31) [Norwegian]
   Brandal, Peter Petersen (age 26) [Norwegian subject]
   Hancock, Violet Beatrice (age 40)
   Johns, Alice Louise (age 20
   Johns, John Herbert (age 24)
   Smith, Pauline Evelyn Augusta (age 67)

12 October 1940 - 'Died at Trafalgar Square tube station' (City of Westminster):

   Woodward, Hilda Irene (age 26)

Turnpike Lane – 5 January 1941

The CWGC records the following as the result of an as yet unidentified incident:

13 January 1941 - 'Injured 5 January 1941, at Turnpike Lane tube station; died at North-Eastern Hospital' (Municipal Borough of Tottenham):

   Foot, Arthur Henry (age 66)

Appendix 1 References:
1. http://www.pollytech.co.uk/wimbledonsa/News%20letters%202003/Oct2003/Oct03.htm
2. PRO HO 186/639
3. Graves, 47.

Below: Two more of the public information posters which appeared in the trains.

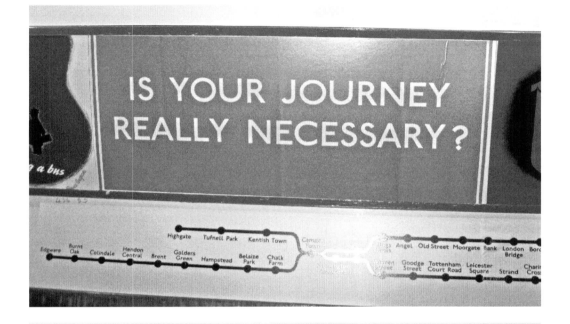

The substantial flood-gates sealing the passageway at Charing Cross (now Embankment) station, which can be seen in situ.

Appendix 2

THE THAMES PROBLEM

At the time of the Munich Crisis (see Chapter 2), LPTB chief executive officer Frank Pick outlined the threat to the most vulnerable parts of the Underground:

> The East London line is an old brick tunnel with very little cover in the river and therefore is vulnerable. It is not possible to undertake any protective works in connection with this tunnel having regard to its age and construction. It is therefore proposed to discontinue the operation of the East London line in air raids and clear all people out. Tunnels also cross the river near London Bridge. Here we are advised that there is 25 feet of clay above the tunnels and while this is not complete cover it is thought that we are justified in taking the risk of continuing to work the railways under the river without special precautionary measures, and this will be done. Tunnels also cross the river at Charing Cross. Here there are four tunnels, two for the Bakerloo Line and two for the Hampstead Line. All the tunnels are practically in the bed of the river. It is estimated that there may be ten feet of mud above them but certainly no solid earth formation. These tunnels are therefore thought to be vulnerable and we are advised that a large explosive shell with delayed fuse action falling between a pair of tunnels might have the effect of destroying both with the result that the inrush of water would be uncontrollable.

Because water would flow unimpeded between lines via cross-passageways at stations, the Northern line would be flooded from Tooting to just short of Camden Town (both branches), the Piccadilly between Barons Court and King's Cross, the Central between Liverpool Street and Notting Hill Gate, and the Bakerloo from Lambeth [North] to Oxford Circus. In addition:

> ... between the District Railway and the river, between Westminster station and Blackfriars Station there is practically no more than the Thames Embankment wall. If this wall is ruptured the District Railway fills as between Barons Court and Mansion House. The water reaches a dangerous depth from Blackfriars to South Kensington. It is impossible to determine how quickly the water would come in. It is thought that the District Railway

must continue in operation in ordinary course but it is proposed to establish arrangements by which, on an air raid warning, the railway ceases to work between the points named. There will be some risk of people being caught between these points if the warning is not ample but this risk would seem to be one which must be accepted.[1]

A hasty decision was taken to plug the Charing Cross tunnels with concrete, with a press statement issued that the Strand, Trafalgar Square, Charing Cross, and Waterloo stations would close for 'urgent structural works,' with *The Times* reporting:

> The effect of these alteration is that there will be no Tube services between: Piccadilly Circus and Elephant and Castle on the Bakerloo Line; Strand and Kennington on the Northern Line. The following stations will be closed: - Bakerloo Line – Trafalgar Square, Charing Cross, Waterloo, Lambeth North, and Elephant and Castle. Northern Line – Charing Cross, Waterloo, and Kennington (Charing Cross side).

After the Crisis was over, the concrete plugs were removed, but then reinstated on 1 September 1939, pending the installation of proper flood-gates. These were interlocked with the signalling so that once an air raid warning had been received, no train approaching the Thames could proceed past the flood-gate ahead of them, while any train that already had, needed to be clear of the first flood-gate on the other side before it could be closed.

This still left the tunnels themselves vulnerable and it was a constant concern for Lt. Col. A. H. L. Mount, the Chief Inspecting Officer of Railways at the Ministry of Transport (see previous chapter). Each time there was damage to a land-side tube, it emphasised that even a near miss in the river bed would be enough to flood a nearby tunnel, but the most graphic illustration had already happened.

On the night of 9/10 September, the schooner *Seven Seas* – moored on the north-east side of Hungerford Bridge – was rocked by the detonation of a 50 kg High Explosive (HE) bomb that landed in the river. The crew reported that, 'the water appeared to spout up for some 30 seconds after the explosion,' caused by air escaping from the disused Charing Cross loop (see Chapter 1), and it was later discovered that water was seeping through the bulkheads installed when the tunnel was decommissioned.

Soundings were taken of the river bed on 18 September, revealing that the bomb had exploded almost directly over part of the loop, about 60 feet from where it joined the southbound running tunnel, causing a crater 5 feet high around its edge, and 15 feet deep in the centre. As the crown of the tunnel was only some 12 feet below the river bed, this meant that the bottom of the crater was actually inside it, partially filled with clay and other debris.

On 20 September divers examined the crater and found 12–15 feet of the tunnel had been fractured. A considerable quantity of ballast and mud was lying inside to a level of around 3–4 feet above the original track level and the loop between the bulkheads was completely flooded. It was realised that another bomb landing in the vicinity could cause a 'water hammer' effect through the flooded tunnel that would easily breach the bulkheads, flooding the southbound running tunnel, and also the District line via a ventilation shaft linking the loop to the sub-surface tunnel above.

It was decided to use divers to build a wall of concrete bags inside the breach in the tunnel, after which the crater would be partially filled with ballast and then capped with a layer of clay. At the same time, a disused passageway connecting the northern end of the northbound tunnel to the other side of the loop was waterproofed, as were original bulkheads and a new one was added to provide additional protection to the ventilation shaft.

As the number of incidents in which tube tunnels were damaged by bombs even falling some distance away increased, so did Lt. Col. Mount's concerns. At the time the practice was to close the floodgates protecting all the sub-Thames tunnels during an air raid, but despite the near catastrophic experience with the loop, it was being suggested that the tunnels at London Bridge, being much deeper below the river bed, were less at risk and so could be kept open. Mount was emphatically opposed to this:

> It is clear that the additional depth of the tubes [at London Bridge] does not justify differentiation from the procedure agreed for the Charing Cross and Waterloo floodgates. The Inspecting Officers are not carrying out their normal functions in this respect. They are normally the Minister's technical advisers on all railway matters; but backed by their knowledge and experience of the last two years, they are in a better position than anyone else in this Ministry to advice the Minister upon the risks which should justifiably be taken in a matter of policy of this kind, and they have no-one upon whom their responsibility can devolve.
>
> It is easy to be wise after the event and say that a risk might safely have been taken after no bombs had fallen during any particular Red Warning; but this Ministry will be hard put to it to find an excuse if, after having spent many thousands of pounds towards making the Tube system safe for transport purposes, the floodgates which have been provided at London Bridge are not used, and the Tube system is flooded in consequence and put out of action for the rest of the war, not only for transport, but even as refuges, together with the almost inevitable loss of many thousands of lives.[2]

Some time after the end of the London Blitz, Dr E. W. J. Phillips of the Experiments Department of the Ministry of Home Security was tasked with analysing tube tunnel damage to date. His final report, dated 26 March 1942, concluded that barring a single outlier, the degree of such damage could be reliably predicted based on both the size of the bomb and its distance from the tunnel itself and could be categorised thus:

Category 1 – Segments of the tube lining fractured and displaced with consequent fall of earth or debris.
Category 2 – Segments cracked or fractured but not displaced sufficiently to allow debris to fall.
Category 3 – Tunnel shaken; rendering and filling cracked, but no segments cracked.
Category 4 – No damage.

A 250 kg bomb exploding within 40 feet of the tunnel would cause Category 1 damage, compared to an Anderson domestic shelter being 'substantially undamaged' at only 20 feet. The chances of each Category of damage being caused were calculated as:

Category of Damage - Number of Cases						Category – Percentage Chance of Damage		
Distance (ft)	*1*	*2*	*3*	*4*	*Total*	*1*	*1–2*	*1–3*
0–20	6	1	0	0	7	86	100	100
21–30	4	1	0	0	5	80	100	100
31–40	2	6	0	0	8	25	100	100
41–50	0	0	1	0	1	0	0	100
51–70	0	0	3	5	8	0	0	38
71–100	0	0	2	15	17	0	0	12
101–130	0	0	1	11	12	0	0	8
131–162	0	0	0	14	14	0	0	0

Phillips noted that casualties were only encountered in three cases of Category 1 damage to platform tunnels, while two hits on station buildings resulting in deaths attributed to people sheltering in ticket halls and on escalators, which gave, 'relatively little protection.'[3]

As the Blitz and intensive bombing seemed to be over, these concerns – although remaining – seemed largely academic until the arrival of the first V-1 flying bombs on 13 June 1944. A hastily commissioned risk assessment from the Research and Experiments Department concluded:

> On the basis of the first eight days of raiding the highest density of flying bombs in any borough has been 0.560 per square mile per twenty-four hour period.
>
> With this density one of the four Charing Cross tubes may be expected to be breached once in every 875 days, i.e. if raiding is maintained for three weeks the odds against a breach occurring are no more than forty to one.
>
> If a breach occurs when the [flood-]gates are open, it is stated by Ministry of War Transport, a length of fifty-seven miles of tube, which may contain sixty – 100 trains, and up to a maximum of 80,000 passengers, it is likely to be flooded.
>
> On the other hand, if the gates are shut, during the whole of one peak period, it is estimated that the war effort may lose about 30,000 man-hours. In addition, tube travellers will be endangered by having to travel on the surface during the firing.[4]

These concerns increased with the advent of the V-2s in the September, owing to their larger warhead and deeper penetration resulting from the much higher impact speed. As

Top: Electrically-operated sliding flood-gate to seal a running tunnel near the Thames. Lower image shows the simpler manually-operated 'diaphragms' used elsewhere.

Surviving flood-gates at Moorgate ....

... and Holborn. And shown below, remains of the flood-gate at Embankment station (Bakerloo Line platform).

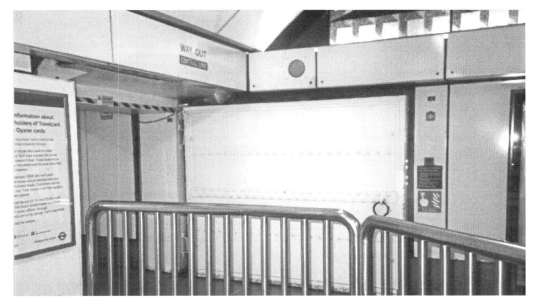

with the way of bureaucracy, being a problem involving water, on 2 January 1945 it was passed from the War Cabinet to the Admiralty, who came up with a novel if somewhat Heath-Robinson solution.

The Admiralty proposed mooring a number of LCTs – of which there was a surplus – directly over the bulk of the Bakerloo and Northern line tunnels at Charing Cross, including the disued loop. On top of each craft, scaffolding would support a 170 x 120-foot rectangular shield made of corrugated iron, each of which would slightly over-lap that on the adjacent craft. The iron would be enough to detonate the V-2's warhead at a sufficient height above the tunnels – even at low tide – that damage would be avoided. Twenty-seven LCTs would be required in all, eleven for each pair of tunnels and five for the loop. One memo warned:

> The scheme at present under consideration does not provide any additional protection to the part in the navigational channel, where the water is deepest. Although a mobile craft might be introduced as a removable defence, the time taken to establish the protection and to free the gap for navigation would be likely to cause undue interruption in the river traffic. To rig a suspension defence to give a minimum clearance of 30 feet above the water at all states of the tide would require substantial towers which might have to be built up from the river bed.'[5]

The 'suspension defence' does not appear to have been investigated to any great detail, but seems to have been predicated on the basis of it being a standard anti-torpedo net strung across the river at high-level. In addition, at an early stage it was suggested that concrete Phoenix caissons – as used to make the artificial D-Day harbours on the Normandy coast – should be used, but this was rejected due to their size.

The final LCT scheme was passed to the Paymaster General for consideration at the end of January, but ultimately seems to have come to nothing. As it was, the V-2 assault ended on 27 March, anyway.

Appendix 2 References:
1.   CAB 21/773.
2.   MT 6/2766.
3.   HO 196/11.
4.   HO 192/36.
5.   ADM 1/19030.

During the war LT staff raised the full cost of two Spitfires, which proudly bore the house emblem – literally – to new heights.

Metropolitan Line train derailed by bomb damaged track.

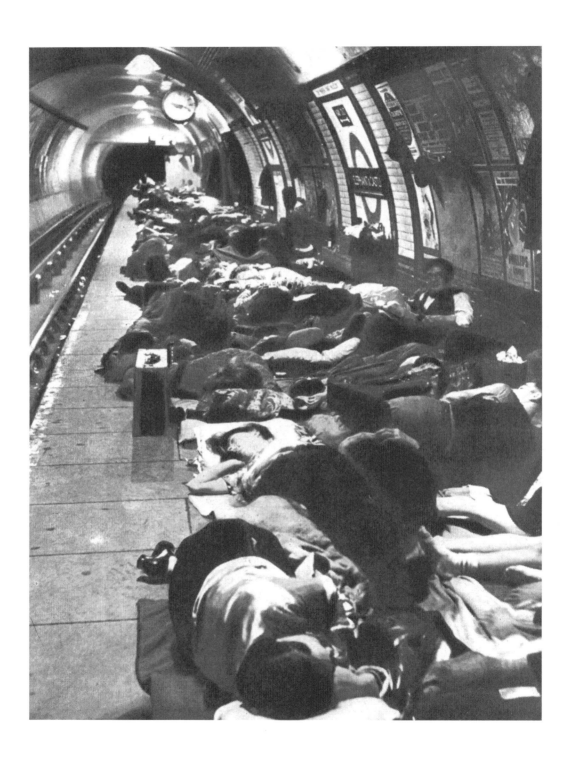

BIBLIOGRAPHY

Works Consulted:

Abercombie, Professor Patrick, *Greater London Plan 1944* (London: His Majesty's Stationery Office, 1945).

Badsey-Ellis, Antony, *The Hampstead Tube* (Harrow: Capital Transport, 2007).

Badsey-Ellis, Antony, and Horne, Mike. *The Aldwych Branch* (Harrow: Capital Transport, 2009).

Bancroft, Peter, 'The Railway to King William Street and Southwark Deep Tunnel Air-Raid Shelter.' *Underground* (London Underground Railway Society – April 1981), pp. 1–29.

Beard, Tony, *The Tube Beyond Edgware* (Harrow: Capital Transport, 2002).

Blake, Jim; James, Jonathan, *Northern Wastes* (London: North London Transport Society, 1987).

Brooksbank, B. W. L., *London Mainline War Damage* (Harrow Weald: Capital Transport, 2007).

Carpenter, Barry, *Piccadilly Line Extension – The Diamond Jubilee* (London: Piccadilly Line (East), 1992).

Croome, Desmond F., *The Circle Line* (Harrow: Capital Transport, 2003).

Croome, Desmond F.; Bruce, J. Graeme., *The Twopenny Tube* (Harrow: Capital Transport, 1996).

Clayton, Antony, *Subterranean City* (London: Historical Publication, 2000).

Conner, J. E., *London's Disused Underground Stations* (Colchester: Connor & Butler, 1999).

Connor, Piers. *Going Green* (2nd edn, Harrow: Capital Transport, 1994).

Croome, Desmond. *The Piccadilly Line* (Harrow: Capital Transport, 1998).

Davis, G. H. (art); Anonymous (text). 'Private and Public Air Raid Precautions: Government Shelters; Group-Refuges for Finsbury.' *The Illustrated London News* (18 Feb 1939), pp. 238–239.

Day, John R., *The Story of London's Underground* (London: London Transport, 1979).

Another view of the Stairway to Heaven memorial at Bethnal Green station, with the entrance down to the Underground station on the right.

Belsize Park south entrance.

Day, John R.; Reed, John, *The Story of London's Underground* (8th edn, London: London Transport, 2001).

Gregg, John, *The Shelter of the Tubes* (Harrow: Capital Transport, 2001).

De Grineau, Bryan (art); Anonymous (text). 'Car Parks and Offices Guarding an Air Raid Shelter for Ten Thousand: An A.R.P. Idea.' *The Illustrated London News* (5 Nov 1938), pp. 830–831.

De Grineau, Bryan (art); Anonymous (text). 'The Car-Park or A.R.P. Shelter: A Project for London's Squares.' *The Illustrated London News* (31 Dec 1938), p. 1241.

Demuth, Tim. The *Spread of London's Underground*. (Harrow: Capital Transport, 2003).

Dunne, L. R., *Tragedy at Bethnal Green*. (London: The Stationery Office, 1999).

Emmerson, Andrew, 'The Plessey Tunnel Factory.' *After the Battle* 139 (2008), pp. 32–43.

Emmerson, Andrew; Beard, Tony, *London's Secret Tubes*. (Harrow: Capital Transport, 2004).

Gibson, Guy. *Enemy Coast Ahead*. (London: Michael Joseph, 1946).

Gilham, John C., *The Waterloo & City Railway*. (Usk: Oakwood Press, 2001).

Goss, Chris, 'The 'Tip and Run' Raids.' *Britain at War* 78 (October 2013), pp. 50–55.

Graves, Charles, *London Transport Carried On* (London: London Transport, 1947).

Horne, Mike, *The Bakerloo Line* (Harrow: Capital Transport, 2001).

Horne, Mike, *The Metropolitan Line* (Harrow: Capital Transport, 2003).

Horne, Mike, *The Piccadilly Tube* (Harrow: Capital Transport, 2007).

Horne, Mike; Bayman, Bob, *The Northern Line* (2nd edn, Harrow: Capital Transport, 1999).

Langdon-Davies, John, *Air Raid – The Technique of Silent Approach* (London: Routledge, 1938).

Langdon-Davies, John. 'Against Epidemics No. 1' *Picture Post* (16 Nov 1940), pp. 18–19, 37.

Langdon-Davies, John. 'Against Epidemics No. 2 – War on Lice.' *Picture Post* (23 Nov 1940), p. 2830.

Leboff, David, *London Underground Stations* (Addlestone: Ian Allan, 1994).

Leboff, David, *The Underground Stations of Leslie Green* (Harrow: Capital Transport, 2002).

Longworth, Philip: *The Unending Vigil* (1967 rev. edn reprint, London: Leo Cooper, 2003).

Mortimer, Gavin, *The Longest Night* (London: Weidenfield & Nicolson, 2005).

Ogley, Bob, *Doodlebugs and Rockets* (Westerham: Froglets, 1992).

Oughton, J. H. (art), Illustration of public air raid shelter under Hyde Park (unknown publication, 1938).

Ovendon, Mark, *Metro Maps of the World* (2nd edn, Harrow: Capital Transport).

Ramsey, Winston G., 'The Secret Underground Railway Executive H.Q.' *After the Battle* 12 (1976), pp. 36–41.

Rose, Douglas, *The London Underground – A Diagrammatic History* (8th edn, London: Douglas Rose, 2007).

The surviving fragment of City Road station, still retained for ventilation purposes (the brick extension above the 'pillars' is a post-closure addition).

Unpublished Sources – The National Archive, Kew, London

ADM 1/19030: Protection of river bed from rocket attack. War Cabinet's proposals for a Bursting layer over Thames Underground railway.

AN 2/1104: Railway Executive Committee, Daily Reports Part 10, 1940.

AN 2/1105: Railway Executive Committee, Daily Reports Part 11, 1940.

AN 2/1106: Railway Executive Committee, Daily Reports Part 12, 1940.

AN 2/1107: Railway Executive Committee, Daily Reports Part 13, 1941.

AN 2/1108: Railway Executive Committee, Daily Reports Part 14, 1941.

AN 2/1109: Railway Executive Committee, Daily Reports Part 15, 1941.

AN 2/1110: Railway Executive Committee, Daily Reports Part 16, 1941.

CAB 21/773: Use of underground railway stations as air raid shelters.

HO 186/321: Shelters, Use of tube stations during air raids and improvement of shelter position in London.

HO 186/639: Air Raids, London Region: enquiry into Bank tube station bomb incident.

HO 192/8: Damage to underground railways.

HO 196/36: Vulnerability of tube railways to attack by V weapons.

HO 196/11: Notes on damage to railway tunnels by high explosive weapons Section 1. Tube railways. Author: Dr Phillips. No. 151.

HO 201/2: Key Points Intelligence Directorate, Reports and Papers, Daily Reports, September 1940.

HO 201/3: Key Points Intelligence Directorate, Reports and Papers, Daily Reports, October 1940.

South of Redbridge station, the heavy-goods shaft opposite Danehurst Gardens.

Sub-surface line today – behind the infamous fake facade of 23–24 Leinster Gardens, Bayswater.

HO 201/4: Key Points Intelligence Directorate, Reports and Papers, Daily Reports, November 1940.

HO 201/5: Key Points Intelligence Directorate, Reports and Papers, Daily Reports, December 1940.

HO 201/6: Key Points Intelligence Directorate, Reports and Papers, Daily Reports, January 1941.

HO 201/7: Key Points Intelligence Directorate, Reports and Papers, Daily Reports, February–March 1941.

HO 201/8: Key Points Intelligence Directorate, Reports and Papers, Daily Reports, April 1941

HO 201/9: Key Points Intelligence Directorate, Reports and Papers, Daily Reports, May–June 1941.

HO 201/10: Key Points Intelligence Directorate, Reports and Papers, Daily Reports, July–August 1941.

HO 201/14: Key Points Intelligence Directorate, Reports and Papers, Daily Reports, January–June 1943.

HO 201/16: Key Points Intelligence Directorate, Reports and Papers, Daily Reports, January–June 1944.

HO 201/17: Key Points Intelligence Directorate, Reports and Papers, Daily Reports, July–December 1944.

HO 201/18: Key Points Intelligence Directorate, Reports and Papers, Daily Reports, January–July 1945.

MT 6/2759: Damage – Underground Railways. File No: ZR.5/79/5.

MT 6/2766: Damage – Underground Railways. File No: ZR.5/79/5/7.

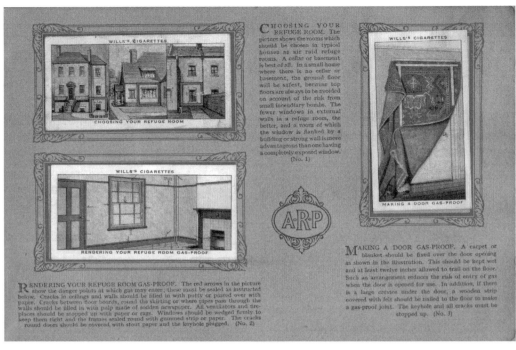

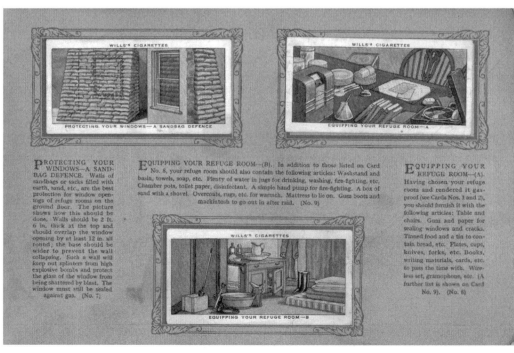

ARP advice in the UK even took the form of an officially-sanctioned cigarette card album from the Wills tobacco company.

ACKNOWLEDGEMENTS

With thanks to Claire Cooper, Ernie Cooper, Robbie Patterson, Frank Rosendale, Sylvia Rothwell and Lilla Sturgeon. Additional images from John Christopher *(JC)* and Campbell McCutcheon *(CMcC)*.

Also from Amberley

Electrifying the Underground
by Graeme Gleaves

London led the world in the development of its subterranean railway system. The first sub-surface lines, constructed by the cut-and-cover method, were operated using steam locomotives. In theory the tunnels and stations were ventilated into the outside air, but in practice they became dingy, miserable, smoke-filled spaces. As one traveller recorded in his journal, 'I had my first taste of Hades today ... the atmosphere was a mixture of sulphur, coal dust and foul fumes'. Accordingly the local chemists enjoyed a thriving business hawking their metropolitan Railway Medicines and potions to the long-suffering travellers.

The railway companies desperately needed to clean up their act. It was only with the arrival of exhaust-free electric traction, combined with improvements to the tunnelling shield pioneered by Sir Marc brunel, that the engineers were able to tunnel far deeper to create the 'Tube' system. It was a public transport revolution.

Graeme Gleaves traces the development of the Underground from the early years and through the introduction and development of the electrified system.

ISBN 978-1-4456-2203-3
£12.99
Published in 2014.